*Make your money by INSPIRATION,
not by the sweat of your brow.*

To F. Y. with all my love.

Acknowledgments

It is impossible to thank all the people who have contributed to this book — but to all of you I say, 'thank you' from the bottom of my heart. Special thanks and love go to my beloved brother Mike Allen who *lives* financial freedom and who inspired me to write this book, Greg Yolen for his beautiful designing and editing, David Heinz for his inspiration and for lending us his wonderful hands for our cover, Ursula Cowan whose honesty helped me to write a better book, Darryl McKinnon whose generous support on every level has changed my life, Maria and David Scaman for being my on-line hand-holders, thesaurus, dictionary and wealth of information about who did what when, Charlie 'Tremendous' Jones who is *awesome* in the way he lives his 'This is it!' and Neil Dooley for his generous and impeccable proof-reading. There are so many more: those who described to me how they achieve financial freedom, those who wrote me off as a failure and fired me with the ambition and courage to prove them wrong, and all the people who so generously donated their stories to make up this book. My eternal love and thanks go to Dr. Jeremy Russell and. Mr. David Povah who were *always* there for me. *I thank you all.*

Touchstone Publications

www.You-Have-What-It-Takes.com
E-Mail: Julia @ You-Have-What-It-Takes.com

First published in The United States in 1999, by
Touchstone Publications
Copyright © Julia Hastings 1996

ISBN 0 9520282 9 8

Cover by Greg Yolen
Cartoons, typesetting and book design by

Touchstone Publications

REAL MONEY

The Art Of Financial Freedom

Julia Hastings

Touchstone Publications

Born in California, Julia Hastings is a psychologist, broadcaster, speaker and author specializing in coaching the art of Mental Picturing. Her books and audio tapes have been translated into seven foreign languages. Julia works one-to-one with the top level business people of multi-national companies and leads regular seminars for people from all walks of life. For more information write to Julia at:

Touchstone Publications

www.You-Have-What-It-Takes.com
E-Mail:
Julia @ You-Have-What-It-Takes.com

CONTENTS

Chapter One   The Wealthy Person's Secret 3

Chapter Two   Live Within Your Means & Dream..9

Chapter Three   How Do You Do It? 25

Chapter Four   Create What You Want 45

Chapter Five   Change What You Don't Want.....73

Chapter Six   Get Rid Of 'The System' 91

Chapter Seven   Back Up Your Success.................109

Chapter Eight   Wealthy People's Secrets 119

Chapter Nine   Treasure Island 131

Chapter Ten   Brainwash Yourself 141

Resources 148

The world is at your feet.

Chapter One

The Wealthy Person's Secret

You can achieve financial freedom and the peace of mind this brings. The key to financial freedom is to make your money by *inspiration* not by the sweat of your brow. This is the wealthy person's secret. It's the inspiring way to make *real* money. Money you *earn* and have a *right* to keep. You owe it to yourself to master this skill.

Get Out Of The Sweat Shop

There are three main ways to earn money. *They all make you sweat.*

First, you can work in a job where you're bored to pieces and know the only reason you got the job in the first place was because you could be hired cheaply, not because you were valued. People 'behind the counter' often feel this way. They sweat for fear they may stay trapped behind the counter forever and never get a chance to live an easy life.

The second way to earn money is to join a large organization; for example, the telephone company. You get better pay and a chance to work yourself up the ladder, as long as you adopt their 'culture' and take on their identity. The only problem is, if you 'make waves' with new ideas or put one foot out of line you could lose your job. You inwardly sweat and watch your step.

Sweet Sweat

The third way is to break away and work for yourself. This is when you'll make money by your *own* inspiration not through the sweat of your brow. You'll make money from your own 'bright ideas' that others may dismiss as foolishness. Your 'bright idea' can be something new to do, or a fresh, new way to do what you're *already* doing. You'll still sweat though. In fact you'll sweat *bullets* when you go out on a limb and do your own thing, because you could fail.

The person 'behind the counter' could fail too if they become so bored they start insulting the customers. They're going to get 'the sack'.

So could the fellow working in the large organization if he pushes his ideas about how something could be done in a whole new, efficient way that annoys his boss. Employed people can fail just as easily as you and I can lose our shirt. The difference is: you're investing your energy in your own dreams, not someone else's.

Believe In Your Dreams

Think of any rich person you admire. Are they doing their own thing or someone else's? Do they look bored and burned out or do they have a sparkle in their eye and a spring in their step?

Eleanor Roosevelt said, "The future belongs to those who are willing to believe in the beauty of their dreams." Believe in your dreams! They're *not* a never-never land you escape to when you need a break from reality. They're the doorway to a new lifestyle. Believe in your dreams and *act* on them.

This is the way to make *real money*. Not fake money, not borrowed money, not plastic money but money you earn and have a *right* to keep. This will give you the financial freedom you've dreamed of. This book will show you how to take your dream of financial security out of never-never land and make it a reality. Starting right now, you'll achieve this step by step. The first step is to start thinking realistically and decide who is in control. In the next chapter you will see how I was *catapulted* into doing this.

You Can Do Fine

You can take care of yourself much better than anyone else can. The only times you'll have financial difficulties are when you buy into the idea that others can do it for you. The price tags on get-rich-quick schemes, 'friends' who *invest* money for you, free, cheap or easy money offered by credit card companies and other financial institutions are just *too high*. I've learned the hard way and just don't fall for them anymore.

This doesn't mean that I don't keep my books straight and pay my bills. I do. *(I had become lazy about this)*. Nor does it mean that I don't use credit. I do this too. But when borrowing I have two golden rules: 1) borrow only to achieve my long term important goals and 2) borrow as little as possible and pay it back *as fast as I can*. I do work that deeply inspires me and live in a place I can *afford* that nurtures my family.

If that means eating scrambled eggs instead of dining out, buying used furniture instead of new, or even living *without* furniture for a while, that's fine. For me, being in debt is the pits. I've been there and never want to be there again.

How Do You Get Inspired?

The way you achieve financial freedom is to *live within your means and dream.* Dream *big* dreams, *huge* dreams. The *bigger* and *more huge* they are the more inspired you'll feel. This is your one way ticket to success. Inspiration is like money in the bank.

If you're in a financial hole right now you can dream your way out of it. In this book, I'm going to show you how I and others have dreamed our way out of hopeless situations and created a whole new lifestyle. We have dived into work that we love and earned money we keep. The way we did this is through a technique called Mental Picturing.

Metal Picturing is a simple mind skill where you see what you want so vividly that you will automatically realize what you need to do to get it. It is so simple even children can do it.

I longed to live in that cottage with all my heart.

Chapter Two

Live Within Your Means & Dream!

Two pits of coal were staring at me. Even in the dim, morning light I could see them. They had stared at me all night long as I tossed and turned in that rack of a bed. Even in the *dark,* I could see them. And I could tell they were not happy with me.

Dash, my beautiful Golden Retriever, who had never known anything but dog-luxury — rides in the front seat of a big comfortable car, running free in the countryside, swimming in lakes and rivers and enjoying beach combing *(where she never missed an opportunity to roll in dead fish)* — had not taken her eyes off of me all night long.

I shifted, my back was killing me. I looked around at the tiny basement room we were living in. Paint peeling off the walls, freezing cold, no hot water and a bathroom that seemed *miles* away. This was our new home.

Dash's puppy Sandy, was sleeping soundly, oblivious to the fact that the three of us were trapped in this horrid place. So much for beach combing and free runs. We were in the 'Big City'. This wasn't a dream, it was a living nightmare come true.

What made it worse was, I knew I was *completely* responsible for it.

I had been living in a fantasy world and had bought into a get rich quick scheme and bought on credit. Like an ostrich who puts it's head in the sand, I had waited too long to *honestly face* my financial situation and take control of it.

When you're driving your car and see a truck stopped in front of you, if you don't put on your brakes you'll crash. Well, just like a driver who wasn't paying attention, I didn't see, no *refused* to see the crash coming. I didn't crash my car, I'd crashed financially. I was penniless and had to start over.

Easy Money?

All my financial problems started when I began buying on credit. That was when I started living beyond my means in order to impress other people. I wanted things to 'look good' *right now.* Cars, televisions, stereos, a more expensive looking house and so on. And credit was so *easy*, all I had to do was take out a plastic card and sign. In came the new television, stereo, holidays and the rest.

My Story

I want to tell you my personal story in order to share with you the nothing-short-of-miraculous-way I came back from a no-hope situation, to be recognized and respected again by people I looked up to (who had written me off as a complete loser).

I am writing this book for two reasons. First to show you how to use Mental Picturing for your own life and free yourself from a system of red-tape that can make you feel hopeless. Second, to show you that the *biggest* lesson I learned was that I *never* needed to crash in the first place.

There was always a way out. The opportunities were always there to get back on track, to become financially secure and have peace of mind again. But I didn't see them or, if I did, wouldn't pay attention to them. To do so would mean I'd have to get out of never-never land, roll up my sleeves and do something about them.

Mental Picturing is what saved me from a near fatal crash and moved me, sometimes by quantum leaps to financially breathing easy again and having genuine self-respect. Self respect that did not depend on what others thought of me, but what I thought of myself. I got so I liked myself and it felt good.

It's Never Too Late To Start Over

This is how it went. At a point in my life just when I was ready to retire, I lost my shirt financially. And when I say I 'lost my shirt' I mean it *literally*. I had to sell all my shirts, blouses, other clothes, linens, pictures off my walls, furniture, china, silver, pots and pans, you name it. I lost everything when the stock market crashed, but I needn't have.

Two weeks before the stock market crash, my son who invested and followed the stock market closely, telephoned from Brazil and said, "Mom, sell all your stocks and shares NOW. I have a bad feeling about the market". I said "Oh no, Greg. Everything will be fine. Those are good stocks and shares. You've got to believe in your decisions". Two weeks later, the market crashed and obliterated my investments. Something else happened too.

"I'll Make You Millions"

At the time I didn't know the ground rules of financial freedom and had lent a hefty sum of money to a 'friend' who would 'make me millions' by investing it for me. I was thrilled at the idea that someone else would invest my money and quickly earn me millions while I sat back and smiled.

You probably know the rest of the story. My 'investor friend' took my money and bought himself a new house, remodeled it and created a lovely garden. I never saw a penny of the money. Even when I had to resort to lawyers to retrieve it, there was nothing left once they'd taken their fees. I was broke, flat broke and had to start completely over.

Jump Ship!

I went into the depths of depression, then one night I had a vivid dream.

I was on a sinking ship, and the captain was *shouting* at me, "Throw everything overboard to save the ship from going under!" I woke up and knew what I had to do. I gritted my teeth and put an ad in the local newspaper to sell the contents of my rented house. I sold everything that wasn't nailed down, except for a few good clothes to wear for future job interviews.

The sale over, I cleaned the house and handed the keys to my landlord. With my two Golden Retrievers, Dash and Sandy, wedged in the back of a little car I'd bought to replace my big one, I made my way to London. I had landed a semi-job there in return for room and board and about $75 a week. My employer expected me to work seven days a week from 8:00 a.m to 11:00 p.m. and only once paid me the agreed $75 a week. As far as board was concerned, forget it.

A Tight Corner

One Saturday after cleaning my little room, I sat on my bed which had a huge hole in the middle but was the only place to sit. A cup of coffee in hand and my two dogs curled up next to me, I had a major panic attack. In utter despair I thought, "How am I *ever* going to get out of this *incredibly* tight corner"? I was still ambitious and had high standards but the possibility of ever being able to live with dignity again seemed hopeless.

I sat there agonizing when a vivid picture came into my mind. I 'saw' a beautiful red brick cottage. It was *absolutely beautiful;* the kind of cottage anyone would want under the best of circumstances.

The cottage I pictured had a lovely walled front garden with a gate and a trellis over the front door covered with Wisteria. It looked like a small perfect paradise. The picture that came into my mind was so vivid that I *couldn't* shake it. It would be a dream come true and I longed to live in that cottage with all my heart.

I Slept In My New House

Every night as I drifted off to sleep, I pictured that cottage, and imagined that I wasn't sleeping in that horrid bed with a huge hole in the middle. I imagined falling asleep, warm and cozy in that beautiful cottage instead. I pictured this every evening and every morning for a week.

I Just Knew What To Do

The following Saturday, exactly one week later, I woke up and just knew what to do. I piled the dogs in the car, drove to the outskirts of the city and I bought the local newspaper. One ad in the 'houses for rent' column immediately caught my eye. It read "Sunny cottage on village green". I knew it was my house. I didn't even read the other ads.

I immediately telephoned and a lady answered whom I instantly liked. I *knew* she would be my landlady. While what she said next was a disappointment, I didn't give up hope. "I'm sorry" she said, "but that cottage has just been rented. But I do have another cottage, it's not on the village green and is only available in a month. Can you wait that long?" Without hesitation I said "yes" and made an appointment to visit her cottage the following Saturday.

A Dream Come True

The following Saturday, as I pulled my car up in front of the cottage, I was so overwhelmed I couldn't get out of my car right away. I just *stared* at the cottage. It was the *exact* cottage I had 'seen' in my mind and had been picturing consistently for a week, only more lovely.

I got out of the car, we introduced ourselves and I walked through the front gate. A little wall surrounded a lovely front garden. A trellis covered with Wisteria surrounded the front door. I gulped and walked into the house, and could barely hold back my tears.

Just For Me

The cottage looked like it had been designed just for me. It was decorated and furnished in all my favorite colors; pinks, greens, creams and soft golds. It was immaculately clean. A soft green carpet led out onto a *beautiful* fenced back garden that was perfect for my dogs. The cottage was situated just minutes from Bushey Park, Richmond Park, Hampton Court and many other gardens where my dogs could have a free run and swim.

My landlady offered me a cup of coffee and we quickly settled the negotiation. The rent was reasonable. No, it was a *gift* compared to other prices. My landlady asked for a deposit, then looked at me and asked, "Can you afford a full months rent? If not I can reduce it", I accepted!

I lived and worked in that cottage for several years building my business and starting my publishing company. My landlady turned out to be one of the nicest people I've ever known. If I needed anything for the cottage, she would give me a blank check and let me choose what I wanted. When it came to paying rent or keeping the cottage up, I never let her down.

Miraculous Breakthroughs

I *knew* it was Mental Picturing that had *flown* me out of that miserable little room into this beautiful spot in record time. Mental Picturing also landed me incredible breakthroughs for work. My financial circumstances couldn't have been tougher, but the breakthroughs couldn't have been more miraculous.

Cold Calling, Warm Reception

Each day I pictured myself making plenty of money. I pictured my bank statement with a healthy balance. Then I got ideas about how to achieve this and acted on them. I got on the phone and started cold calling, never an easy job. But I tried something new. Before making a call I would sit down and picture the telephone smiling broadly. The result? My cold calls were met with an incredibly warm reception.

I immediately landed a job one day a week giving Mental Picturing workshops at the popular Pineapple Dance Studios in London. Next, a smart health club in Chiswick hired me to give workshops to their stressed-out executives. So did a health club in the city. Word quickly spread about what I was teaching and I could not keep up with the demand. I led workshops, offered one to one coaching and gave talks.

People Got Rich

In teaching Mental Picturing a pattern emerged. I realized that everyone I personally coached went on to make large quantities of money and get promotions. I raised my fees. Clients also recovered from illnesses, gained self-confidence and found partners. Once they got the hang of Mental Picturing they couldn't lose for winning. Neither could I!

Winning Streak

This work deeply fulfilled me. Seeing my clients 'take off' when they had been in dire straits gave me a real buzz. Don't forget, I'd been there. Even though I still had far to go, I was on a winning streak. Many clients became good friends.

Yet I was restless to do more. I realized that one to one coaching could only reach one person at a time, but if I wrote books I could reach thousands. I started to write. Later I joined a government program that gave me a small grant to help support it. Mental Picturing had created a whole new life for me and enabled my clients to do the same. Many of my clients now teach Mental Picturing and make a good living at it. You can too.

A New Challenge

Was it all smooth sailing from there? No. I was working extremely hard giving three workshops a week and organizing many full weekend seminars. I was coaching people the rest of the time, writing late into the night and not getting enough rest. I skimped on food too. I thought I could just push through and work on sheer adrenaline, or so I thought...

Knocked Flat

A severe bought of flu knocked me flat but I had a workshop to give. As sick as I was, I thought 'The show must go on'. Dosed with painkillers, I gave the workshop anyway and went home twice as sick. That was the worst flu I've ever had. I recovered, but not totally. Something was different. I was exhausted all the time and one day while buying groceries, I kept dropping things. This clumsiness was unnatural for me. I knew something was amiss.

Day in and day out I was so exhausted that just brushing my hair tired me out. I finally went to my doctor, Dr. Jeremy Russell, my most loyal friend through this tumultuous time.

I said, "Jeremy I am so tired that if wild lions broke through my front door and wanted to eat me, I would just sit there and let them. I wouldn't have the energy to get up and run".

My doctor diagnosed a post-viral syndrome that causes extreme exhaustion. I said, "O.K., how long does it take to get over?" He hesitated then said, "Some people get over it in a few years, others take longer". "A few years!" I gasped, "I don't have three days. If I don't work, my dogs and I won't eat! I've got to get over this NOW!" He looked at me sympathetically. I drove home in shock.

Swim, Dance And Run

As soon as I got home, I let the dogs out in the garden, collapsed on the sofa and said "NO!" No self-respecting person had to put up with this intolerable situation. I started picturing immediately. Even if I *had* been dragging myself around, *nothing* could stop me from using my mind to picture myself running. I was *not* going to be a weakling for three years.

I pictured myself swimming, dancing and running. After picturing I knew clearly what to do. I decided to take massive doses of vitamins, start eating a good diet and arranged to float in a float tank twice a week for one month. I floated in an enclosed tank of warm water saturated with epson salts, which as strange as it may sound, is deeply restful. While 'in the tank' I pictured being strong, radiant and healthy. Every day, morning and evening, I pictured all the things I would do with my new, non-stop energy.

Release

Two months later, I was well. One Sunday I took my dogs on a picnic to Richmond Park, which was situated close to our cottage. We walked the park for hours. The more we walked the stronger I felt. That day my energy returned and with rare exceptions I have never looked back.

I learned the hard way how important physical health is to financial freedom and from then on was careful not to 'burn out'. I learned to stop my frantic pace and make myself lighten up when my energy got low.

Books, Books, Books

I realized that Mental Picturing could be applied to solve *any* problem and went on to write. I pictured my books being read by people all over the world. Since then I've written several books and recorded audio tapes to go with them which have sold in the hundreds of thousands and have been published in seven foreign languages.

I've worked hard and consistently to achieve this success one step at a time. The deep fulfillment it gives me grows every day.

"Dear Julia, thank you for your inspiring books and tapes on mental picturing!"

Edith Iovanella, Topsfield, MA., USA

Own the goose, not just a couple of its eggs.

Chapter Three

How Do You Do It?

This chapter is comprehensive. You can skip straight to page 45 to Create What You Want if you're eager to get started. But come back and read this chapter because it will show you how Mental Picturing works, why it sometimes doesn't work and what to do about it.

Own The Goose, Not Just Its Eggs

I was catapulted into living within my means and not 'keeping up to the Jones'. In fact, I couldn't even *fool* the Jones' anymore, I'd crashed. Yet my miraculous breakthroughs made me *think*. I *knew* something else was at work here, not just 'luck'.

I was *making* my own luck and knew it was my mind, through Mental Picturing, that was responsible for it. I felt like a 'Golden Goose' was working for me.

I decided to *own* the Goose, not just a couple of it's Golden Eggs and never lose it again. To do this, I analyzed, step-by-step how Mental Picturing worked and this is what I learned:

9 Steps To Financial Freedom

1. Take total responsibility for your present financial situation.
2. Start, right now, living within your means.
3. Believe in your dreams and decide what you want.
4. Use Mental Picturing to 'see' yourself having what you want.
5. Act on your ideas about how to make your dreams become real.
6. Put aside false pride and don't be afraid to ask for help.
7. Never give up.
8. Don't burn out.
9. Say "Thank You". All professionals do this and they mean it.

Get Rid Of Your Albatross

Being an ostrich and putting my head in the sand had landed me in a financial nightmare, *(to say nothing of utter humiliation)*. When I took my head out of the sand, woke up and *got real*, I decided what I wanted. Then I pictured *having it* even though it seemed *impossible* under the circumstances. By the way, having respect for myself and being respected by others again was one of my *major* goals. Being treated like a loser, a has-been and a write-off was *the worst* part of my experience.

Beggars Can Be Choosers

The most heartbreaking part was that I had to go 'begging'. When I realized I had absolutely no money left, I asked long-time friends if they would help me start over with minimal loans of $500. All of these friends had enough money to not blink an eyelash at spending $500 on a shirt.

When I asked them for a loan, they dropped me flat and wouldn't speak to me anymore. I didn't exist for them. This just devastated me. Some of these friends had previously asked *me* for loans when I had money of my own. I un-hesitatingly lent them money, but only on one condition: that it was a gift not a loan.

Well, being stonewalled by old, 'loyal' friends was a really hard lesson to learn, but by the Grace of God new, supportive friends appeared in my life who didn't care a bit if I was broke. All they cared about was that I was in there pitching. They generously supported me through net-working and advice. One even paid my rent for a month, when I just couldn't make it. I had a new set of friends. And, after all these years, they're still wonderful friends and the best people on earth. I wouldn't change them for anything.

Yet still, at that time, I *had* to get the albatross of failure off from around my neck a.s.a.p. You may need this too.

Close Your Eyes And Imagine...

Do you feel like a loser?
How does it feel?

Do you want to be a success?
How does that feel?

Which feels better? Being successful or a loser?

A Lovely Home

I wanted a lovely home again. Through Mental Picturing, I dreamed my way into a beauty. But I had to act fast. Before, when I lived in never-never land I would have waited around for someone or something to fly my dream through the window.

Now, the *minute* I got an idea through Mental Picturing about *how* to get something, I shot out of my chair and immediately started pounding the pavements. Not just the pavements, the phone, the library, the press, the radio and any government program that could help me. I didn't have much choice, when you have to jump ship, you don't wait for a helicopter to come by and rescue you, you *jump*. I jumped through quick action.

For example, after picturing that lovely cottage a clear idea came to my mind to get the local newspaper in a suburb of London. It took me about one hour to dress, load the dogs in the car, drive there and buy it. I immediately 'spotted' my new home, found the closest pay phone and enquired. Before, I would have waited about a week before acting. By then, the opportunity would have been snapped up by someone else.

Hope Is Essential

I didn't give up hope when the landlord told me the 'sunny cottage on the village green' was already rented. I felt strongly she would be my landlady and waited hopefully for the 'second best' choice. In my heart I knew the second cottage would be better.

Money

I wanted the dignity of having enough money to be financially free once more. I pictured this consistently, got ideas about how to achieve it and acted on them. I started cold calling and a new career opened up. Almost overnight, I developed a high profile for what I was teaching. Mental Picturing was a unique form of coaching I *knew really worked* and wanted to share with others. I started attracting corporate clients who recommended me to others.

Licking Your Wounds Gets You Nowhere

All I can say is put aside false pride, and don't delay. You just can't afford it. Licking your wounds won't get you ahead. Lick them for a while, but then get moving. Selling all my belongings hurt, but I couldn't eat a valuable porcelain plate. I needed the *cash* to start over.

When you're climbing up the ladder (or climbing back on again) you have to be utterly realistic and prepared to do what you need to do to keep the cash coming in.

In lean times I baby sat and dog sat. Doing small, menial jobs won't diminish your self-respect if you consistently keep your big dreams in sight through Mental Picturing. In fact, work like this will *grow* your self-respect. Better to have money in your pocket and big dreams than no money at all.

Never Give Up Hope

Thanks to Mental Picturing I never gave up hope. There are two main reasons for this. Firstly, when you picture positive future goals you trigger the release of hormones called endorphins. These are the body's natural opiates. No pill or drink can give you this natural, wonderful high. You'll feel hopeful. When you practice Mental Picturing consistently, you will feel this. Everyone does. If you feel low, it's a sign that you've let your picturing drop.

Your Perfect Lover

Second, there's a part of your mind that wants to give you *everything* you want. In fact, this part of your mind wants to give you *much more* than you want. It's called your subconscious mind. Every time you practice Mental Picturing you contact it directly.

Your subconscious mind is the dreamer in you who can make your dreams come true. It's your best friend. It will never let you down and will consistently show you how to have the good life and get out of jams.

Listen...

Your subconscious talks to you *gently* through creative ideas, feelings in your body or dreams. It also talks through others when you'll listen. Let's break it down.

Your subconscious brings vivid pictures into your mind like the cottage I 'saw' while living in that little room.

Your subconscious talks to you through feelings that you're on the right track. It also talks through depression, aches and pains or exhaustion that show you're on the wrong track.

Your subconscious protects you through dreams like the one I had of the sinking ship. Thanks to that dream I used my common sense and sold everything that would give me some cash to start over.

Your subconscious talks to you through others. You can say 'NO' or 'YES'. Remember my doctor who diagnosed three years of recovery? I said 'NO', reversed the odds and got well.

You Do The Picturing, Your Body Acts

Your subconscious is a treasure chest of helpful ideas. Your body does the work. Your mind *(subconscious or otherwise)* does not have hands, feet or a voice that can talk on the phone or make those calls. Your mind can't get-face-to-face with your customer, write a contract or close those sales. Your body does this.

Mental Picturing will give you the courage and confidence to take actions that you once just couldn't face. When you see your actions work out, just like they did for me, you'll never look back. The more you practice Mental Picturing the more you'll experience, *first hand*, the kind of lasting success it delivers.

The Pattern Of Mental Picturing

Mental Picturing will have it's highs and lows. You'll picture vividly and intensely for a while, then you'll begin to feel bored and impatient. Tighten your seat belt, because you're about to be catapulted into tremendous action. Why?

Your subconscious mind has taken the hint and is now delivering solutions in the form of ideas and opportunities to help you achieve your goals. Sometimes people will spontaneously offer you things, but 90% of the time you have to ask people to support you: the press, friends, a company that could give you a job, etc. *Nine times out of ten you have to go to them, they won't come to you.*

Tony landed his sale.

Being A Pest Is O.K.

People will eventually support you, but often you have to be *very, very* persistent and remind them. Paloma Picasso said, "A career doesn't happen overnight. You have to convince people to believe in you". And here she was, the famous artist, Pablo Picasso's daughter, with millions behind her and contacts to match. But she still had to push her vision just like you and I. She made it, not because she rode off her dad's name, but because she had something valuable to offer. She made it, so can you.

Be persistent, even if you feel like a pest, *it doesn't matter.* When you're sincere, believe in your product and have approached prospective customers in a sincere way, they'll sense your sincerity and commit. Tony Allen found this out.

The Story Of A Persistent Young Man

I love this story. It's true. Tony Allen was a salesman. He sold blue jeans in New York's garment district, one of the toughest places to sell in. Tony had an 11:00 a.m. appointment with a customer who had repeatedly said he would buy Tony's great jeans, but so far hadn't. At this meeting, his customer finally said, "Look Tony,

I'm *not* going to order your jeans this time, but I *promise,* the next time you visit me, I'll give you an order. I promise"!

A Good Lunch

They shook hands and Tony walked out of his office and went and had lunch. At 2:00 p.m. on the very same day, Tony walked back into his customer's office. His amazed customer looked at him and said, "Tony, what in the daylights are you doing here again?" Tony replied, "You promised me that the next time I visited, you would give me an order. Well, here I am".

His customer grinned and shook his head. They sat down at the table and Tony got the order. His customer couldn't stop chuckling as he wrote it. According to Tony, it was a *very good* order, not a mediocre gesture. The end of the story is a win-win. Tony's jeans sold well for his customer and they've done steady business ever since. ***Tony's persistence and daring paid off.*** What did he have to lose? He'd *listened carefully* to his customer *(if you don't listen carefully you'll never sell anything).* He seized on his customer's promise and landed the sale. At the same time he gained respect in the eyes of his customer.

Brush Off Rejections

"Life goes to the courageous". Tony had an instinct about how to creatively handle his customer, he seized on it and won. You can too. Once you've got the habit of being persistent, it will become *fun* and you won't take rejections *personally.* You'll learn how to turn them to your advantage, just as Tony did.

If you're sincere, believe in the product or service you're selling you won't mind being persistent. Sell with integrity and inspiration *(which is what Mental Picturing is all about)* and you just can't lose. Remember Tony's story, practice Mental Picturing, and you'll brush off rejections. When you say "yes" to success and believe in what you're doing it will take the sting out of people who say "no".

'Working Yourself Up' Is <u>Not</u> 'Working'

Stress comes from two things: non-action and over-action. Non-action is dreaming without doing. We often get ourselves all worked up about all the work we *could* do, but it ends right there. Procrastinating on important work you need to do won't move you ahead. So, 'get in the saddle' and just 'do it'. You'll feel a lot more confident and in control.

Stress also comes from over-action. This is when you drive yourself mercilessly and don't give yourself a break. You can't think constructively when over-stressed. Nothing will work when you drive yourself this way. So, don't think this next step frivolous.

Lighten Up!

When Daley Thompson won the Olympic Gold Medal for the decathlon he was asked, "What's the secret to success?" His response was simple. Daley replied, "Learn to relax". It's the height of wisdom to lighten-up and relax. You can't afford to be dull and burned out when you're going for success.

As you harness your courage to follow your ideas, doors of opportunity will fly open for you. This can overwhelm you but go for it! Don't stop picturing when opportunity overwhelms you, just scale your picturing down to about three no-doubt-about-it goals you'll always want. Then lighten-up. Lightening-up will refresh you and your relaxed attitude will instil confidence in your clients.

Lighten-up by treating yourself. This doesn't mean going out and buying an expensive television you can't yet afford. It means doing light-hearted things, like going to the movies, watching a video, taking a warm bath while you listen to beautiful music, going on a picnic or sharing a meal with friends.

Lighten-up times will refresh you and get your mind off 'business'. When you stop concentrating on a project and lighten-up then Bingo! The solution you've been waiting for will just pop into place. The telephone may ring and the person you've been waiting for to say "YES" might do so. This is how the hard work you're doing with your mind will pay out. Try it and see, don't take my word for it.

Live With A New Friend

You're going to live with Mental Picturing as a long-term friend. Make this a pleasure. Expect miracles to happen, these are things that turn out better than you expect, like Tony's sale or my perfect little cottage.

The more you picture, the more windfalls will happen and soon you will anticipate them happening. As a result you'll develop a success attitude. Others will notice and want to support you. *Everyone* who pictures *consistently* experiences this.

An Exciting Ride

Is it all smooth sailing? The good news is you won't want it to be. Life will *never* be boring again. Mental Picturing is like sailing a boat. You will have peaks and troughs. Your life will speed up and then slow down. You need to learn how to relax when you hit a standstill and understand why your Mental Picturing sometimes stalls or backfires. When you do, you'll make a friend of Mental Picturing for life. It will always support you.

Taking Risks

To succeed with picturing, you'll become a bit of a risk taker. This doesn't mean taking silly risks like lending money to a 'friend' who'll 'make you millions'. *It means believing in yourself and putting yourself on the line.* You need to follow through on your ideas and try them without *any guarantee* they will work. Gradually you'll develop confidence in your instincts and put yourself on the line. Others will watch as you succeed and sometimes fail. When you succeed they're going to want to know how you did it. If you fail, *so what?* Mental Picturing will keep you feeling confident enough to brush off failures.

Tell other people about your Mental Picturing *only* if you're sure they will completely support you, and then sparingly. What works for you may not work for another. Mental Picturing leads to success, but we each succeed at our own pace. Trust yourself.

Trouble Shooting

You'll achieve so many things through Mental Picturing that you can feel magic. But in other areas you can get stuck. *This is because you always get what you want, not what you ask for.*

You want plenty of money and even though it's one of the easiest things to make through Mental Picturing, you can't seem to get over the hump. Then you finally break through to financial freedom. Why? Why didn't you get it right away? There are two reasons for this. First, you may still believe that depriving yourself of money will make you a better person. Second, you have many subconscious sub-wishes that come into play. Your *strongest* wish will dominate.

Why Money Doesn't Come Easily

Let's deal with your sub-wishes first. Your relationship to money is no different to any other. Think of any happily married couple you know. Did they start out that way? Certainly they started out in love, but their strong, happy marriage is the result of having worked at it consistently *for years*. It's the same with money.

You want money, but your sub-wish wants to learn the secrets that will turn 'earning it' into an *enjoyment* instead of a *struggle or a battle to be won*. When you learn these secrets you'll make money more quickly, easily and enjoyably. We may try get-rich-QUICK schemes, but they hardly ever work.

Give Yourself Permission To Be Free

In cracking your money problem, you're giving yourself permission to be free. Sometimes you and I deprive ourselves of the freedom money can bring for fear we would make fools of ourselves or waste it. Learning how to handle money *elegantly*, and never lose it once we have it is more important to us than having pots of it right now.

One Step At a Time

Another example: if you want to paint beautiful pictures, but you don't know the fundamentals of drawing, you have to learn them. The same goes for money. You have to learn the fundamentals of growing it steadily and consistently. Once you've got the fundamentals under your belt, you can go on to create money until you have more than you need.

"I'd Been Better For Failing"

One of my clients is the retired chairman of a well known merchant bank. As a second career, he set up his own business consultancy and asked me to coach him. I'll never forget what he said. "I wish I'd started up on my own early in life and failed a couple of times. I think I would have had more character, courage and been a better businessman for it.

"What I did, was always go for the security of that paycheck and working my way up the corporate ladder. Even though I reached the top of a world class bank and was envied by others, I think I would have been a richer, more creative businessman for going out on my own and failing a couple of times. If I'd learned from a couple of failures; I could have turned them into a personal victory as well as a public victory".

Why not let Fortune smile on you?

Chapter Four

Create What You Want

There are some people Fortune smiles on. Everything seems to work for them. You can be one of them when you decide what you *really* want. That's what this chapter is for.

You may think it's only money you want, but there's something more. You need to earn money through work that *inspires* you and contributes to others. When you work at something that fires you with enthusiasm you'll still work *like blazes*, but you'll do it because you enjoy it, not out of a sense of struggle or obligation.

The reward is the *deep satisfaction* of doing something you believe in. As a result, you'll create a real *life* for yourself not *'just a living'*. There's no mistaking the sparkle of someone who is doing this. They've found their "This is it"!

On the other hand, if you see work as a struggle, a sacrifice or a battle to be won (*over others*), it takes all the pleasure away. You cannot afford to do work you don't like or believe in; or for that matter work with *people* you don't like. You'll feel trapped and like a martyr. This feeling communicates itself to those around you and they will shy away. Your health, your bank account and *relationships* will suffer as a result.

Inspire Yourself

Don't mix-up selling with inspiring. If you inspire your customers you will also sell to them because it's honest. You must believe in what you do or you won't sell anything. If you give people the hard-sell, or even the soft-sell and are not sincere, they will sense it. They won't cooperate or buy and you'll stay broke.

The only way to inspire your customers is to *inspire yourself first.* You do this by investing your mental energy in your dreams of a fuller, better life. You do this through Mental Picturing. Your 'dreams' will inspire you to believe in a happy, worthwhile future.

When you believe in what you're doing or selling, you'll communicate this to others. Remember Tony and his blue jeans? He believed in his product, and inspired his customer with his sincerity and daring. They both ended up winning

If you already feel inspired, believe in what you're doing, are raring to go, turn to page 58 where you'll find Mental Picturing techniques to create abundant money. But if making money has been a hurdle for you, read on.

Rich, Rich, Rich?

Money gives you the freedom to pursue your passion. It also buys you privacy.

Your passion is what you would do if you had enough money to *never* have to worry about it again. This book will help you earn money, keep it, grow it and never lose it again. To do this you need to understand the difference between being wealthy and being rich. There's a *big* difference.

Wealth

Wealth is something that happens in your heart. Being rich is something that happens in your bank account. If you go for *wealth,* two things will happen, 1) money will no longer be a worry for you and, 2) you're bound to become rich. If you go for just being rich, you'll run the risk of losing it.

Peace Of Mind

Being wealthy is a relaxed state of mind that comes

from enjoying what you do and enjoying life even though there're still things you'd like but don't yet have. When you're wealthy, you have *quality of life*. You're in control and are your own boss.

"I Live Very Modestly"

You can be wealthy even on modest means because you'll enjoy what you have. A highly respected businessman I coached said to me, "I live very modestly. I never spend more than I can *comfortably* earn". He has his priorities straight.

Don't worry. You can be wealthy and rich at the same time. In fact, you can be wealthy on *lavish* means for the same reason. You make the choice and set the pace.

Back To Basics

You'll never become rich and *stay rich* until you've mastered being wealthy first. Why? The first step to being wealthy is to take total responsibility for what you have right now and what you *don't* have. Don't blame anyone else. Just start taking care of what you have right now so you can have more.

Take A Look Around

Take a look around where you are right now and acknowledge, "I have it, I love it, I've earned it and I deserve it". If what you have now isn't enough for you, don't throw it out, damage it, or ruin it. Start up-grading it through Mental Picturing until you can tangibly replace it. When you *appreciate what you already* have and take good care of it, you're bound to attract more. Sometimes you and I have to 'lose it' and 'do without' to appreciate how much we already have.

Too 'Rich' For Your Blood?

Are you living a lifestyle that's too rich for your blood? One you just can't afford, but feel you need to 'look good' in the eyes of others? You're going to have to get *really real* here. You'll never regret this. It will give you a quality of life and control that you'll never give up. Take another look around...

What If You Had The Cash?

How much is the home you're living in right now worth on paper? Are you paying a high mortgage? If you had the *cash* your home is worth, would you live in that same home or buy another?

How much is your car worth on paper? Do you own a luxurious car you're making high payments on? If you had the *cash* your car is worth on paper, would you own that same car or change it for a good used car and use the extra money for something else? Take a realistic look at your possessions and what they're worth.

If you've bought them on credit and had the *cash* they're worth, would you still own them or change them to less expensive but equally serviceable models? This exercise will help you realize your true values. Then you can set some new goals for yourself which are described on page 54.

Rich Overnight?

Being rich as opposed to being wealthy is having masses of money. Not plastic money or credit or promises, but *lovely accessible cash and hard assets you can immediately turn into cash.* Yet, if you don't feel you deserve or appreciate what you have right now, being rich won't make you happy.

You can get rich overnight. This happens. A company skyrockets, someone wins the lottery, another inherits a fortune or a 'poor person' marries someone rich. This is when money seems to fall out of the sky.

The problem is that unless you've learned how to earn, grow and maintain your money *through your own efforts*, you can become broke just as quickly. Newspapers are full of stories of rich people who've 'bottomed out'. Why is this?

Quality Of Life

Wealthy people fill their lives with objects, activities and relationships that bring them pleasure, not ones that impress other people. *Rich* people are usually so busy 'chasing the buck' they don't have time to enjoy what they own. They need more and more and *more*.

Passion

The ability to fully enjoy life whether you're 'working', 'playing', 'rolling in clover' or going through a 'lean time' is called passion. Passion is when your enjoyment springs from within yourself and is not dependent on other people or pastimes to *entertain* you.

Through Mental Picturing you'll develop a passion for succeeding and an enjoyment of life regardless of your circumstances. I know. It gave me a high even when I was living in that depressing basement room. It gave me hope. And my hope turned out. I've seen, first hand, Mental Picturing do the same for countless others. I've seen it *completely* change their lives when they picture *consistently.*

Wealth Is Permanent

Wealth offers a quality of life that is *permanent.* This is another of the wealthy person's secrets. To be wealthy you have to get your priorities straight. You do this by setting clear goals.

You and I never fail because we lack opportunity or ability. We fail because we're not certain about our goals. We make half-hearted attempts to achieve goals we don't really want and then beat ourselves up when we fail or barely scrape by. The truth is, we never really wanted the goal we were 'going for' in the first place. We wanted something else. Discovering this is another key to being wealthy. It's called your "This is it!".

'No-Doubt-About-It'

Go for goals you're absolutely sure about. For instance, "I want a half million in an off-shore savings account by the time I'm 55", or "I want to live in the country where I can breath fresh air and raise my kids in a stable way the city doesn't offer".

Michael Wolff Broke Free

Michael Wolff, 54 and father of two did this. A respected, self-employed businessman, Michael bit the bullet and took a major risk. He moved his family from their smart London home to Aberdeen, Scotland. There Michael set up on his own. He was determined that it would be a fulfilling experience not just financially, but in all of his relationships. He was going for quality of life.

Michael had already worked for himself. His former company, **Lydiastar Telecommunications,** was so successful it was bought out by the courier giant, **DHL.** Michael then joined the London-based **Results Group PLC** as a self-employed consultant. "I helped large corporations empower their staff" says Michael, "but I realized it could *never* be done. When you work for a large corporation, you have to 'fit in' and butter-up the people paying your salary. But if you stand back and ask, "What do I think about myself?" the price-tag to your self-esteem is just too high.

A Better Quality Of Life

"I couldn't hack the competitiveness and 'keeping up with the Jones'. I wanted a better quality of life for my wife Jessica and my two children. I wanted to live closer to nature, have better quality air, less traffic and be free from overcrowding.

"Despite the risk involved, my new Internet company grows every day and my relationships have flourished. Taking this 'leap of faith' involved a *huge* risk but it worked. I'm now writing a book about our experience".

Nothing Will Stand In Your Way

When you're clear about your goals nothing should stand in your way. I say *'should'* because there is one thing that *will* stand in your way. That's your idea that someone else should give you what you want. You give it to *yourself*. Make this decision and you won't fail. Now, set some clear goals for yourself:

Which Goals?

What three things, if you had them would completely change your life?

These are your three most important goals.

Of these goals, which one, if you achieved it, would enable you to achieve your other goals ?

This is your most important goal.

What practical actions can you take right
now to turn your goals into reality?

This is your action plan.

Action

When you've thoroughly thought over your goals, start
taking practical actions to make them happen. Even if
you do one small thing a day, your financial situation
will begin to change. (By the way, playing the lottery,
pools, drugs or booze *don't count).*

What if you worry you don't have the *energy* to
change? Don't. Mental Picturing *gives* you energy, it
doesn't take it. We already talked about how picturing
positive goals releases body hormones that make you
feel enthusiastic and confident. As a result, the changes
you need to make will feel like an adventure instead of
a chore.

What If You Don't?

Let's get real again. Getting real is essential to success.
It means doing what you need to do to achieve your

goals. To pursue your passion, you have to do what it takes to set yourself free. What have you got to lose?

New Questions

What is my life going to be like in 1, 5 or 10 years if I don't get going?

What *could* my life be like in 1, 5 or 10 years if I really put my energy into making my three main goals a reality?

Writing Goals Helps

Writing your goals daily in a special note book will help you become certain about them. As you write you'll know, "Yes, I want this" or "No, this is not that important". As you write, you'll automatically see how to make your goals happen.

Why Not Get Paid To Sleep?

This is another story I love. Vidal Sasoon was a hair dresser in the 60's in Hollywood. One of his best friends was the actor Michael Caine who was his room mate at the time while Michael was trying to 'make it'. Michael watched Vidal cut hair in a frenzy. Vidal was a *genius* at it. Almost everyone in Hollywood wanted him to cut their hair. He was always fully booked and couldn't keep up with the demand.

Leverage Your Talent

One evening Vidal returned home exhausted. Michael said to him, "Vidal, you have one pair of hands and just so many years that you can cut hair. Why don't you combine your talent with hair and create a line of products that will pay you to sleep? Once your hair cutting days are over, you'll have your own products that will give you *recurring income*".

Vidal did just that. He analyzed all he'd learned about hair and capitalized on his image with the 'high and mighty' in Hollywood to launch his own products. While he cut hair, he marketed his products. His customers eagerly bought them. His fame spread and he took off! Vidal created a comprehensive range of *quality hair products* and other spin-off products.

Vidal Listened

Vidal had the ability to *listen* to great advice. He spotted a Golden Opportunity to leverage his talents and grow a sideline of products that more than paid him to sleep. He made millions!

Pull A Rabbit Out Of A Hat

Now, here are some Mental Picturing techniques. Yes, this is a book about earning money. But *in your imagination, you're going to have it the easy way.* The picturing techniques in the rest of this book will move you into financial freedom and get the boredom out of your life. Mental Picturing makes earning an adventure and *a lot of fun.* Doors of opportunity are going to fly open. You may be surprised how quickly. When those doors fly open, rush into them. Try this:

"I Need It NOW!"

Let's say you need money *fast* but it seems impossible. Your need is *not* impossible for a magician. And that's what you're going to become through Mental Picturing: *a magician of your mind.*

You may need to pay a huge bill, or have a project you want to finance, but raising the money seems about as easy as pushing a huge barrel of water up hill. Why not try pulling a rabbit out of a hat? This is what one of my clients did and it worked.

"After agonizing and pacing the floor day and night, I decided nothing but a miracle would help", my client said. "But that's exactly what I decided to pull off. I sat down, closed my eyes and imagined I had a magician's top hat in my lap. I reached in with both hands and imagined stroking the rabbit's soft fur. Very gently, I lifted 'my miracle rabbit' out of the hat.

Pure Relief

"I pictured the words 'Unlimited Money' written on it's fur. In my imagination I held my rabbit close and felt it snuggle even closer. I pictured this scene morning and night and *felt the pure relief* of having the financing now. I pictured for about four days and suddenly got an idea. I decided to call my bank manager and ask for a line of credit. I told him what it was for, and to my utter amazement, he readily gave it to me. I didn't have to go on bended knee or even visit his office. I was stunned.

"I got the money, the project came off without a hitch and I was able to pay back the money very quickly which put me in a good light with my bank. Now, when I need credit, they're always supportive. Even today I'm amazed at how easy it was. I'm convinced it was 'The Rabbit Technique' that did it".

Rake It In

They say money doesn't grow on trees but in your imagination it can. Imagine this powerfully enough and mouth watering windfalls will come your way.

Relax, close your eyes and imagine you're in your own private orchard. It's a beautiful balmy autumn day and the leaves are falling, except that instead of leaves they're $50 bills. You have a wheelbarrow and as the leaves fall, you rake them in. *Smell* the scent of crisp new bills, *feel* the pleasure that they're *real money* not checks. You rake them in and put them in your wheel barrow in *huge armfuls*. Miraculously they all fall into place in neat stacks. The raking is easy. The bills are light and crisp. They *smell* wonderful and *feel* great to the touch.

Breathe Deeply

As you pick up huge armfuls of *real money*, hug them close, *take a deep breath* and *smell* your armfuls of money. Then put them in your wheel barrow and rake in another armful. Then another, and another.

When your barrow is full, wheel it to your home. Be sure to look over your shoulder at your orchard of trees, bursting with money leaves and money that covers the ground. There's enough money there to keep you in clover for the rest of your life. And it's all yours. *Feel* the pleasure.

Now push your wheel barrow to your home where you have a special 'money room' and place all the crisp, new cash in neat stacks on the shelves. Your room looks like a library, except instead of having books on the shelves it has neat piles of fresh, new bills. The room smells wonderful. Stand back and look at your money room and think, "Soon, I'll need another, larger room to store all the money from my trees".

Go back to your orchard, rake in more money until you feel satisfied. Then stop. Remember, this is your orchard and they're your money trees which are in *perpetual bloom.* Affirm, "I have unlimited access to money, all I have to do is rake it in".

Soft Touch

It doesn't 'rain' money, so they say. But in your imagination it can. Hail falls from the sky on a beautiful day, why not money? Try this: relax and picture yourself outdoors on a beautiful day. Suddenly you feel a 'soft touch' on your shoulder, then another on your hand, then your cheek. You feel gentle 'soft touches' more and more. Where are they coming from?

You look around and see money floating down from the sky all around you. You can hear a gentle sound like leaves falling in the wind. You look down and see that $100 bills are falling on the ground all around you.

You look up in amazement to see that money *really is* falling out of the sky just for you on this beautiful day. Crisp new bills and neatly bound stacks are covering the ground like a thick carpet.

You happen to have a couple of large carry alls with you. You open them and start filling them with the money. There's enough money in them to buy you anything for the rest of your life. Affirm, "I have enough money to last me forever. All I had to do was pick it up. It was *free*".

Genie Can Do

Here's another. Imagine that one day you're out shopping with no particular purchase in mind. You're just browsing. You walk past a junk store, stop, look in the window and out of curiosity decide to go in. You never know what you might find. Actually you don't expect to find anything special, but you think "Well, why not just browse around"?

The shelves and tables in the store are full of an assortment of things, old books, bottles, dishes, clocks, silver, you name it. Something on one of the shelves catches your eye. It's an old brass lamp. The kind you read about in fairy tales that you rub until a Genie comes out.

What A Lamp

The lamp's dusty and tarnished, but it has a certain charm. "Give it a little polish" you think, "and it could really look good". On an impulse you decide to buy it.

You negotiate with the proprietor who gives you a very reasonable price, wraps your lamp in newspaper and hands it to you. You put it under your arm and take it home. *Your Magic Lamp.*

Upon arriving home, you look your lamp over, take out the brass polish and begin polishing. It polishes easily, and actually the brass underneath has a lovely luster.

Whoosh!

You're polishing away, when 'Whoosh!', out emerges a Genie. You think you have lost your marbles! Out of your little lamp emerges this incredible Genie, who gets larger and larger. You sit there, transfixed, eyes wide open and mouth agape. Once out of the lamp, the Genie stands back and smiles at you. He's gorgeous, just like the Genie in fairy tales, well built, lustrous, tanned skin with a turban on his head. You stare...

Then your Genie speaks: "Hello, I've been waiting for someone to discover me and let me out of this lamp". He says, "I'm at your service". He gracefully bows to you and repeats, "Your wish is my command, how can I help you"?

At Your Service

When you can finally speak you gulp and say, "Are you *real*"? Your Genie smiles, nods his head and says, "I certainly am, and I'm at your service. Just say, and I'll give you anything you want". You take a deep breath, shaking your head, still wondering if you're losing your marbles. Your Genie benignly smiles at you and repeats, "Name anything you want".

You take another deep breath and say, "Well, actually there *is* something I'd like. I'd like a pot of gold". No sooner do you say this, than with a sweep of his hand your Genie produces a huge pot of gold. Beautiful golden coins overflow in a large antique pot. You see these coins are pure gold, *the real thing*, the *finest* quality gold. Stunned, you swallow and simply say "Thank you". Your Genie smiles back and asks, "Will that be all for now, or would you like another wish"?

Thank Your Genie

You reply, "No, that's more than I could ask for right now. How can I thank you"? Your Genie replies, "You don't need to thank me, it is I who should thank you. I am at your service and have been waiting for a chance to give you anything you want. Any time you want anything, just rub the lamp and I'll be happy to give it to you".

Stammering a little, you thank your Genie again, "I really don't know what to say but thank you". Your Genie smiles warmly, bows and says, "Just remember, anytime you want anything, no matter how large or small, just rub the lamp and I'll be here for you". With that he magically returns into the lamp, which in the meantime has become completely lustrous and requires no more polishing.

You examine your pot of gold. It's the finest gold you've ever seen, in a quantity that must be worth *millions.* Still stunned, you run your fingers through the gold and can't believe your luck. Your heart fills with gratitude. *Feel* this now and say "Thank you". Continue to *feel* your immense gratitude as you affirm, "I never have to worry about money again".

The Genius In You

Just remember, the Genie you released from the imaginary lamp is the 'Genius' you're going to release in yourself through Mental Picturing. You'll see.

Win The Lottery

Who doesn't want to win the lottery? It always tickles me when I coach business people who, even though very successful and wealthy, still would like to win the lottery, just for the fun of it. I do too. Who wouldn't? I only buy a ticket when I feel inspired to, because I refuse to get 'hooked'.

Have you ever noticed the people who line up at the supermarket to buy lottery tickets, especially on Saturday? Most all are on the survival line. Yet I've won small amounts and it's fun. These small wins don't make me go back for more, they make me feel lucky.

Odds Are Better Than Lightning

When business people state they'd like to win the lottery, I tell them to go for it, but explain carefully how it almost always plays out. Yes, they *could* win an amount on the lottery, but studies show that the odds of winning the lottery are even less than being struck by lightning. What *always* happens as a result of *picturing* winning the lottery is that you'll get fired-up with new creative ideas about how to make more money, work more creatively, or motivate your staff. Either way you 'win'.

Feel The Thrill

Now, sit down, get comfortable and picture winning! Imagine you've won the jackpot, and feel the *incredible* thrill of it. What would you do with the money? A swimming pool? Imagine swimming in it. Imagine giving gifts to friends, perhaps handing each an envelope full of cash. A new car? Imagine you're driving it. Then affirm, "Winning is great! I can't lose for winning". Now act on your ideas about how to make money more easily and really enjoy it.

The End Of The Rainbow

We are taught as children there's a pot of gold at the end of the rainbow. You may say that's nonsense, but the rainbow's real, so why not the gold? Standing in an imaginary rainbow is a great money technique.

It's especially helpful to forget missed opportunities. How often have you looked back and kicked yourself because you missed a great opportunity? We've all done this. Without realizing it, we *were* at the end of the rainbow and didn't realize it.

Stop Seeking And Find

The rainbow's end and the pot of gold can be yours

right now. You just don't see them. We're so used to searching and striving for the rewards of life that we never let ourselves enjoy what we've achieved. Enjoy the rewards you've worked for *now*. Stand in a rainbow.

Relax, close your eyes and imagine you're standing at the end of a beautiful rainbow. Look down and see there's a pot of gold under your feet. Hear and feel the gold crunch as you shift your weight. Know you've reached the end of the rainbow and that finally the pot of gold is yours.

A Mattress Of Money

You can also imagine that you're sleeping on a bed of money — fresh, new money. The bills are stacked evenly side by side on a king-sized bed. They're so comfortable to lay on they're like a water bed or a really comfortable air mattress. As you roll over, they roll *with* you. If you've slept on a waterbed or air mattress, you'll know how fun it is. The mattress shifts with your weight. Imagine you're sleeping on one now.

Smell the fresh, new money you're laying on as you drift off to sleep picturing those neatly stacked bills spread out all around you. Run your fingers over them and feel the unmistakable texture of money. Affirm: "I have as much money as I could ever want. It feels *wonderful*". Don't be surprised if you have a vivid dream about how to increase your income. That's your subconscious talking to you. Act on your inspiration.

Let Fortune Smile On You

There are some people Fortune smiles on. All the lucky breaks come their way. They attract opportunities and money like a magnet. And, what's more, they don't strive for it. It seems to come to them effortlessly.

You can become one of them. Try this: imagine you're out on a beautiful day: you can be taking a walk, sailing your boat or driving your car. Or, you could be sitting in a restaurant having a cup of coffee with a friend. Next, imagine a bright warm sun is shining down on you. This is the sun of Fortune.

Feel it's warmth flooding through your body and know that it's filling you with plenty of energy that will bring you good fortune and good luck. Picturing this, and *feeling* it will give your subconscious mind the message that 'Fortune' is now on your side. Several things can happen: you could have a 'win' of some sort, a large win, or an unexpected positive change could happen in your life. *You might even realize that what you want most deeply you already have*. This will bring you peace of mind. Affirm, "I give myself permission to stop struggling and let Fortune smile on me".

The Way It Feels Right To You

Change *any* of these picturing techniques to suit yourself. As you picture, you'll get many ideas about new, creative Mental Picturing techniques *of your own*. Remember the only 'right way' to do Mental Picturing is the way that feels right to you. Enjoy!

Pull the rug on the rug puller!

Chapter Five

Change What You Don't Want

One of my favorite Mental Picturing techniques is also my *most* controversial. I teach people how to get rid of what they don't want.

In the next chapter on page 91 you're going to get rid of the *biggest* thorn in your side and that is 'The System', or 'Big Brother' whichever you want to call it. If you want to skip ahead and read the next chapter right away, it will fill you with power. But the chapter you're reading now is full of Mental Picturing techniques to help you change what you don't want.

Some people think that changing, getting rid of or even destroying what you don't want is negative. I spoke at an international seminar in Greece on positive thinking and the audience almost *stoned* me when I taught them to do this. They thought I wasn't spiritual enough or was being too negative.

All I can say is that *the most dangerous toxin in the world* is repressed anger. Why on earth should you live with this burden?

Repressed anger turns into resentment, self-pity, antagonism, manipulation, self-punishment, guilt, blame, self-deception, etc. *All* of these can turn into poverty and debilitating diseases. You can't afford to entertain anger. It ruins your mind and your body. *Let it go!*

A Battle?

Sometimes you just have to 'do battle'. People let you down, sell you short, steal from you or break you with criticism. You just can't take it. But don't worry, through Mental Picturing you can 'have it out' in your mind in a *clean way*. The harmonious results you'll experience will be nothing short of miraculous. I know this first hand.

Have A Heart-To-Heart In Your Mind

We all get angry. If we say we don't, we're only fooling ourselves. Anger is a natural and powerful emotion. If used in a beneficial way, it can be turned into something positive. Yet, we all *dread* confrontations. They're not easy. We'd rather keep everything on the surface nice and friendly, even though we're smoldering and hurt inside.

You don't need to have a face-to-face confrontation with the person your angry with if you'll have a heart-to-heart talk with them in your mind. You may be surprised how serene and positive you feel after having a 'mental' heart-to-heart. You'll release dangerous, explosive anger and get your relationship back on an even keel. Just try it and you'll see. Try this:

"This Is How I Feel"

Relax, close your eyes and get *really* relaxed. Next, imagine you're sitting with this person. Tell them *honestly* how you feel, what it was they did or said that hurt you or let you down. Imagine you're both talking calmly, each telling your own side of the story. Picture sincere understanding on the face of the person you're talking to and *feel* it on yours.

Next, picture both of you getting up to shake hands, or give each other a hug. Hear the person you've just 'had it out with' apologize and say, "I never saw it that way, but now I understand and I'm sorry". In your imagination, you do the same. It takes courage to apologize. Some people never do it. They're always right. But an apology is not a sign of weakness, it is a sign of strength. And, it will make *you* feel a lot better.

Time Is Money

Once Mental Picturing has become a habit you will develop steady self-confidence because you'll be accustomed to succeeding. Your attitude will change accordingly. Your time will become *very* valuable to you. You won't waste it. When you've reached this point, instead of 'talking behind another persons back' or 'gossiping'. You'll confront difficult situations directly and with courage, just because it needs to be done. You won't feel the self-defeating desire to blame anymore either.

Go For Respect

As you succeed, you'll also become frank. Not in a hurtful way, but you'll just 'tell it like it is'. If someone treats you without integrity, you won't say, "Oh, don't worry, it doesn't matter, it's alright", when it's *not*.

Instead you'll clearly tell them how you feel, that it is *not* O.K., you're disappointed and why. It won't be pleasant, how could it be? But you'll respect yourself for your up-front honesty and they will too. We all want to be liked, but remember when it comes to having people like you or respect you, *go for respect*. They'll end up liking you as well.

Never An Argument?

Sorry, but sometimes you're going to blow up. Things just go too far. You may have to face breaking up a relationship. It happens in marriage, business and almost every other part of our life.

When you come to this point *you'll know*. It's inevitable. If you'll do some Mental Picturing first you can end the relationship in a friendly way. Then when an argument happens, you can handle it (as much as possible) in a fair way without a lot of blaming. There's a bonus, you may even up-grade your relationship to a new, more supportive level.

When ending a relationship, whatever it's nature, do it as nicely as you can. Of course it will hurt, but look at it this way; if a relationship has been draining and paining you, when you end it all you're losing is pain. Keep this in mind and it will give you heart and the courage to start afresh.

Inner Strength

Through Mental Picturing you'll develop an inner strength that's very up-front and fair, not only with others but with yourself. This takes time to develop, but it will happen, be assured. Until you reach this point, you need techniques to get rid of what you don't want. This can be poverty, illness, a difficult co-worker, shyness, or your failure syndrome. These techniques will work for anything you need to get rid of.

Money Is As Plentiful As Air

This book is about *you* having money. Money is an energy. It is as plentiful as air. But just like air, it can't flow to you if your mind is all clogged up. Think of your mind as a filter or a screen. If they're all clogged-up, fresh, new positive ideas can't get through.

Clean That Screen!

Haven't we all seen window screens that are so full of lint and dust the air just can't get through? Well, imagine you're like a screen. If you want money to flow easily to you, you need to clean the screen of your mind. Try this:

Picture a screen, perhaps one of those lift-off screens for a window. Picture it so clogged up with lint, dust and dirt that you can hardly see through it. In your imagination, take the screen out of the window, set it in your garden, get a garden hose and turn it on. Now start *gently* squirting your screen until it's spotless. You may need to get some detergent and a brush to get it really clean.

When you've finished, stand back and look at your perfect, clean screen, then place it back in your window, sit down and *feel* wonderful fresh air flow and waft all around you. Affirm, "Money now flows to me as easily as fresh air. My mind is open and clear".

If you practice this technique don't be surprised if you get all fired-up and want to clean your office, sort your files, end a depressing relationship, clean your car, or start jogging regularly. There're many things that clog our energy and slow us down. These are a few you may think of when you 'clean your screen'.

Crack The Nut

This is another favorite of mine. I practice it *very often.* It's a winner. Crack the nut.

Who hasn't cracked a nut? Cracking nuts in your imagination signifies solving a difficult problem: something that's been on your mind, or a stumbling block you just can't get over. Crack the nut of struggle, poverty, debt, rejection or *anything* that's bothering you. You'll live a much more positive life when these burdens are gone. All you need are some imaginary nuts and a nutcracker.

The Nut Cracker

At Christmas and New Year's, we eat walnuts. After all the feasting is over, we sit around the table, talk and pass around walnuts and tangerines. We all crack nuts. Especially walnuts. Sometimes nuts crack easily, other times they're a little messy. But it's a lot of fun. I love cracking nuts as Mental Picturing techniques. They're easy, effective and feel *really satisfying*.

You May Need A Sledge Hammer

Picture several nuts, I enjoy picturing walnuts because they're the biggest and easiest to crack, but you can go for a coconut if you want. Crack one nut at a time or line them up. Let's say you line them up.

Relax, close your eyes and picture your nuts with the words poverty, debt, struggle, 'just can't win', loser, loafer, failure, you name it, printed on each nut. Then take out an imaginary sledge hammer and one by one 'let 'em have it!'. Take careful aim and crack your nuts one after another.

I mentally crush my nuts on a little cement walkway outside my back door. I line them up and picture the problem I'm trying to 'crack' written on them and then crack each one. My walkway can be cleaned easily; hosed down, swept up or even vacuumed. (I wouldn't *consider* letting those negative nuts inside my house).

As I *wham* each nut, I take careful aim and *feel* the impact of hitting it straight on, flattening it and *feel* the pleasure of knowing I'm rid of that problem. Then, in my imagination I either vacuum up the remains or hose them away.

A Pile Of Money

Sometimes I picture the nut's 'remains' magically disappear to be replaced with a huge pile of money. I pick up the money and take it in the house. The walkway is left clean, pristine and perfect.

This 'clean end' delivers a positive message to your subconscious mind. Don't leave an imaginary 'mess' behind. Clean up your 'nuts' (or, let your *Genie* do it for you). Then replace them with wealth, freedom, ease, winner, success and so on. Enjoy the feeling of *being* all these things *right now*. Then affirm "I succeed in every way", or "I can't lose for winning".

This technique will work quickly on how you *feel*. You won't feel out of control or helpless any more. You'll start to get ideas about things you can do to get rid of your problems. Coincidental lucky changes will happen too. Here's another cracker technique.

Become A Safe Cracker

You may have a problem on your mind you just can't figure out how to handle. This can be a difficult co-worker or someone you love you just can't get through to. It may be a negotiation you're trying to complete, or simply your worry about how to make ends meet. Become a safe cracker and you'll solve your problem.

Most of us have opened a combination lock. This can be a wall safe, a bicycle lock or one on a briefcase. But it's fun, turning the dial back and forth to the right numbers until it clicks into place and the lock opens.

Open Sesame

Let's imagine you're opening a wall safe or a vault, the kind you've seen safe crackers open in movies. Open the door that conceals the safe, spin the dial, then carefully start turning the dial right and left, right and left, then give it a final turn to the right and feel the dial click and stop. Turn the handle and *feel the pleasure* as the heavy door soundlessly swings open.

Inside is the solution to your problem. It may be stacks of crisp new money, a pouch full of perfect, polished diamonds, other precious gems or simply an envelope with the word 'Solution' written on it.

If you get an envelope, open it, take out the paper inside and read *the solution*. You don't need to know what the solution is right now, this inspiration can come later. Just take out the envelope, 'read' your solution and *feel* the relief of having the perfect solution to your problem. Affirm "My problem is now solved, I've found the *perfect* solution".

Now drop your Mental Picturing and wait for the answer. An idea will come to you about how to solve your problem. Bingo, suddenly, you'll just know what to do. And you'll smile.

Get Off The Win-Loss Syndrome

How often do you earn money, or get out of debt and start to feel secure when something comes along? It could be a big, unexpected bill, or your pet might need an operation, or you might need expensive dental work, or the central heating blows up, or you skid on black ice and the car needs a big repair. Suddenly your newly acquired financial security is blown. Just as you were back in the black, you get the rug pulled on you. (We'll deal with the 'Rug Puller' on page 87).

Pleasure Brings Balance

Without realizing it, a lot of us have a win-loss mind-set. This is because we believe that our money should go for 'needs' not enjoyments. We earn money to survive and dream of the day when we can have the ease of wealth. Deep down, we don't believe it. We believe we have to struggle to make ends meet and that all our money should go for survival. *If* and *when* we get lucky, then we can splurge on enjoyments like a holiday home, a boat, a great car or a cruise.

"What goes up comes down", "The higher they rise the harder they fall", "Life goes in peaks and troughs", are sayings we believe. Believing these can turn your life into a roller coaster ride of getting ahead only to fall back. You can change this. Life can go in a circle too. A *winning circle* when you change your mind-set.

This is how you start: when you make a financial win, immediately go for another. You may not make big wins, but consistently stacking up small wins will train your mind into a new habit of positive expectation.

Reward Yourself

When you land a big sale, get back in the black, or meet a tight deadline no matter how difficult it was, reward yourself. Don't take all the money and pay off your credit cards or the mortgage first.

Take a small portion of the money and do something special for yourself or your family. Buy yourself a gift, for example some clothing, like a track suit you've wanted but haven't wanted to spend the money on. Take a weekend break with your family or friends, go out for a meal or buy yourself the bicycle you've wanted.

Just be sure when you make a win to reward yourself, not *after* you've paid all the bills, but first. The reason for this is simple. If you reward yourself last, your subconscious mind gets the idea that you don't count much and that your obligations count much more. How disheartening! Feeling this way will only invite more obligations into your life.

Don't Go Crazy

Your obligations and commitments *are* crucially important, but so are *you*. You deserve to treat yourself when you've made a win. *Just keep it in proportion.* Don't go crazy and blow all your profit on pleasure, or you'll dive into guilt when there isn't enough left to pay down the mortgage or your credit cards. This will make you feel like a loser.

Get Off The Win-Loss Roller Coaster

In another of my books I mention a roller coaster technique. I want to repeat this image in a new way. Relax, and imagine you're on a roller coaster, one of those super-duper one's that climb way up and dive way down. Picture it painted in a *dreadful* colour and see the name 'Win-Loss Syndrome' painted on it's side. Imagine you've finally come to a stop at the platform where you can get off. Don't hesitate! Get off the Win-Loss roller coaster as fast as you can and let the others continue. Then walk over to The Continuous Win Carousel and leap on.

Continuous Win

As you leap on this lovely carousel, sit in a booth, on one of the carousel ponies, or imagine getting up while the carousel moves in a graceful circle to beautiful music. Imagine wandering in and out and trying all the different rides as the carousel gracefully turns in a circle. *Feel* the pleasure of trying each ride.

As you drift off to sleep at night, or even for a short cat nap, imagine you're through with the Win-Loss Syndrome and have chosen the Continuous Win Carousel forever. *Feel the relief* as you fall asleep.

Don't be surprised if you get an unexpected win of some sort that has nothing to do with hard work. That's a sign that your subconscious has taken the hint that you're now open to some mouth watering windfalls to come your way. Others get them, why not you? Affirm: "I've now chosen The Continuous Win as a new way of life and will follow my hunches about how to make my new attitude permanent".

Get Rid Of The Rug Puller

Now let's get rid of the naughty Rug Puller. The Rug Puller is a ghoulish creature that should be *permanently demolished*. He's the one that always spoils the fun. Just when you've landed that big sale, he does something to take the fun out of your new found wealth or win. He's a *no good spoil sport* and you need to get rid of him. Demolish him or better yet, pull the rug on *him.*

Try this: picture a miserable little Scrooge-like creature standing on a rug in your family room. He doesn't belong there. Sneak up quietly behind him, grab the rug firmly and give it a strong tug. *Wham!* See the Rug Puller land flat on his back, (or backside). Picture him furious at having the rug pulled out from under *him*.

He'll Never Come Back

Next picture him get up, dizzy and red in the face from embarrassment and watch him walk off in a huff. Hear the Rug Puller say, "I'm getting out of here, this place is the pits. I'm *never* coming back".

Well, your home may be 'the pits' for the Rug Puller, but it will be *Heaven* for you once he's gone. Feel the pleasure of knowing the Rug Puller is out of your life forever and will never come back. Affirm, "The Rug Puller is gone from my life and can never spoil my fun any more".

Go For The Magic Carpet

You can also picture the Rug Puller change his attitude. Sinners become saints all the time. So can the Rug Puller.

Once you've pulled the rug on him, picture the Rug Puller get up, pull himself together and turn around and apologize. Hear him say, "Look, I'm really sorry. I misunderstood you. I thought you got a kick out of having the rug pulled from under you. Now that I know you don't, I'll help you turn your life into a Continuous Win".

'See' real sincerity on the Rug Puller's face and picture him transform into a nice looking fellow. Imagine he puts his arm around your shoulder and walks you over to a magic carpet which you stand on together.

Feel the magic carpet lift off and fly you both to an Aladdin's cave of wealth, riches and happiness. When your carpet 'touches down' in the cave of riches, *see* the Rug Puller roll up the carpet and give it to you as a gift. *Hear* him say, "This is my gift to you. A Magic Carpet. It's yours forever".

Get Rid Of Your Mental Obstacles

When seemingly *insolvable* problems are facing you, remember, there's *always* a solution. It's just that we get so involved in and feel so hopeless about our problems, we can't see a solution that is sitting right under our noses. Getting rid of what you don't want works fast to clear away obstacles to creating what you want. Once you try them, you'll use them with confidence.

Send 'Big Brother' packing.

Chapter Six

Get Rid Of 'The System'

This chapter will show you how to get out of financial jams and understand why you got there in the first place. Take heart! In the next chapter we'll review simple secrets to help you become wealthy and stay wealthy *for life*.

What I am going to say now is not an indictment on *'The System', 'Big Brother'* or local or national governments, the telephone company, gas or electric companies, banks, financial institutions or credit card companies in particular. But open your eyes and stop being 'Sold'.

Sleight Of Hand Selling

Governments and large conglomerates make their money by sleight of hand. They use a stacked deck, and the deck is stacked in their favor, not yours. *'The System'* or *'Big Brother'*, whichever you want to call it does not want to take care of *you*. It wants you to take care of *it*. Large conglomerates don't really want to serve you, they want you to serve *them*. Their object is to keep you dependent and spending to keep *them* wealthy, not you. To achieve this they tell you half the story, confuse you with their terminology and hide behind small print.

How often have you bought computer equipment only to find that to make it work you need to buy more? How often have you claimed on 'best buy' insurance or a 'guarantee' to have the company discover some technicality that lets them off the hook and you holding the bag? How often have you tried to get a walkman or answering machine repaired only to find the repair cost is as high as buying new? How often have you been lied to by sales people or have them treat you coldly when you return something? This is sleight of hand selling.

This also happens on a small scale. A friend of mine Jack, described how his father used to sell aluminum siding for houses. His dad said the price depended on "what the customer was foolish enough to pay".

If big institutions or shady 'business people' are giving you the runaround, selling you to distraction, harassing or short-changing you, you've bought into their multiple services and products that promise to take care of you and save you time and money. You pay their bills (sometimes *for years)* to find you've received nothing in return but an overly complicated life, high overheads and their continual demand for *more*.

Cut Them Out

Take your independence back and as much as possible *cut them out of the picture.* The only things you need to succeed are a telephone, answering machine, fax, dependable car, a set of decent clothes, and a basic P. C. to write letters on — all of which you can get second hand. You're going to 'go lean' and you'll love it.

In this chapter let's explore some eye-opening facts so you can start saying 'No' and keep what you earn.

1999

A recent poll in The United States revealed that people unanimously want three things:

1. A good job.

2. Less taxes

3. And above all, <u>*to be left alone*</u>.

You may feel the same

The Oldest Trick In The Book

The key to achieving financial freedom is to get rid of 'The System' or 'Big Brother'. Do you really believe that large banks, organizations and governments want you to be wealthy? Of course they do, because they want you to make *them* wealthy.

They do this by the oldest trick in the book. They pretend to be your friends when all they want is your money. To get your money they seduce you through sugar-coated marketing that makes you believe if you buy their multiple products or services, the sky's the limit. *Don't believe it.*

Their real goal is to turn you into a number — a customer who will automatically give them your money with no questions asked. Yet there are many people who don't buy into this. But these courageous individuals sometimes pay a high, humiliating price.

Fingerprinting

Let's take one example. John, lives very simply by choice. He works and pays for all of his needs in cash. He doesn't have a bank account or owe money because he wants to live a simple, red-tape free life.

For years John brought his employer's paycheck to a huge U.S. conglomerate bank it was drawn on to have it cashed. This worked until 1997 when the bank instituted a 'thumb print signature program' for anyone who was *not* a customer of the bank and wanted to cash one of the bank's checks.

Now, every time John wants to cash his employer's check he has to go through the humiliating experience of being fingerprinted. Do you think John is being treated like the hard working, honest human being he is, or is he being treated like number?

The Law

When John was told that in future he would have to be fingerprinted he objected and asked to speak with the bank's manager.

A senior manager approached him with a "pasted on smile" and said, "Tell me your problem. I am here to help you, but you must understand we have to protect our customers. If you were a customer of the bank, you wouldn't have to be fingerprinted. Would you like to open an account with us? We'd be happy to serve you". Tom declined and weekly, ever since he has to go through the humiliating process of being fingerprinted in order to cash his employer's check.

John overheard one of the bank's senior manager's say to one of the teller's, "Yeah, it's just like 1994 and 'Big Brother' now".

Manipulation Is Big Business

John did his homework. He learned: "The law states that a check is the same as *real money*. It's cash. It is a demand for cash and must be paid in cash if so demanded. Not so for this huge bank. They have made their own rules that penalize and humiliate anyone who is *not* their customer. Should you give in, or should you stand fast as John does? If we stand fast and group together we can stop being manipulated.

Tracked Like An Animal

Darryl McKinnon, 34, is a former IRS agent and father of two. He says, "Banks and the government discourage the use of cash because credit and ATM cards are very profitable to them. First, they can track you like an animal and analyze your spending habits. Then they make money by selling your name to companies who inundate you with tele-sales and junk mail".

"The IRS Turned Me Into A Monster"

Darryl understands 'The System' as no one else does.

Make your money by INSPIRATION...

Darryl used to work for the IRS, the equivalent of the Inland Revenue in the U.K. In any country: 'the tax-man'. "When I came home from work one evening and realized my own daughter was afraid of me I quit. The IRS was turning me into a monster".

Darryl was one of the the IRS' top men, yet by choice he now works from home as an independent financial advisor. He also runs his own publishing company producing self-help manuals to help people understand their rights and become financially free. Darryl also helps clean the house, prepares supper and takes care of his two daughters while his wife works outside the home. They are a close-knit, happy family who pull together.

"I Was Selling Hopelessness"

"The IRS trained me to believe I was providing hope to people. Actually I was giving them a feeling of hopelessness and helplessness. I saw people come into my office, especially women, so terrified they couldn't speak. When I raised my concerns with the IRS, no one could tell me with a straight face *how* I was actually helping these people. I knew it was wrong. What they wanted me to do was manipulate people and I just couldn't live with it. I quit".

Marketing The Kids

One of the fastest growing markets in the States (which is quickly spreading into Europe) is marketing to young kids because they have a large amount of disposable income. Young people are now seen as tomorrow's consumers. Surveys show that they have 14 billion dollars a year to spend. Fifteen year old's now have credit cards.

Corporations target young people for their disposable income and because they're the most vulnerable. They're naive and impressionable. The idea is that if a company gets you while you're young, you'll develop 'Brand Name Loyalty' to their company, their products and probably stay with them for life just out of convenience.

You're Not Told The Whole Story

Darryl McKinnon clearly understands this strategy, with an MBA in marketing and experience in a major consumer products company he says, "Companies sell you multiple products and services by telling you what you want to hear, not *the whole story. There is a lot of misinformation that is legitimized* by organizations and the government who 'sell' irresistible products and services for a 'peanut' on the promise that they will save you time and money.

"But when they sell, there's a catch. They tell you the benefits you'll get, and leave out the real cost. Not telling the whole story is part of their strategy to hook a new customer. Misrepresentation and non-disclosure is how they make their money. If you knew the real price, you would never buy their products in the first place".

Say 'No' To The System And Win

Fortunately, there are consumer organizations that will support you if you're up against a giant (or a cowboy) who is taking advantage of your trust. *(See resources on page 149 for lists of helpful books and organizations).*

The Better Business Bureau in the U.S will point you in any helpful direction. In the U.K. you have the Citizens Advice Bureau that helps people know their rights. Every country has organizations to support the consumer. Use them when someone takes you for a ride. It can be hard work, but it will take you out of victimhood into power. *I have never known a wealthy person who paid an unfair bill.*

Get The Facts Before You Buy

Knowledge is power. It will help you say 'No'. This is

one thing I never deny myself anymore and that is taking professional advice. I learned this wisdom at a seminar. One of the speakers was an accountant who coached us about how to handle money and make our business succeed. He said, "Take advice. *If you think advice is expensive, try ignorance*"!

That really hit home because I was so ill informed about the real financial facts about how to grow money instead of spend it. Ever since I have taken plenty of advice when making an important decision. Yes, it costs in time, energy and money, but it has saved me thousands and thousands of dollars and brought me tremendous *peace of mind.*

Taking advice means informing yourself about what things really cost, how to run your business, how to write contracts that protect you, keep your books straight, work out repayment plans for your debts and get collection agencies off your back.

Collection Agencies After You?

Tell them to 'cease and desist'. This is a standard letter that protects you by law from being harassed by collection agencies, so if you have a grievance with a company who is hounding you for money you have *the legal option* to tell the collection agency to get out of the way and work out your grievance directly with the company.

No matter what your financial situation is, there are many things you can do to take the upper hand when you're being harassed by unscrupulous organizations who hide behind small print to legally *steal* from you.

Stay On Top Of The Books

The accountant on the seminar I attended said something else that made an indelible impression on me. He said, "If you stay on top of your books you can keep the control". I never forgot it because not staying on top of my books had landed me in a mess.

Ever since, I've kept my books straight and as soon as I could afford it, got myself a good bookkeeper, an accountant, and planned a strategy for paying off my debts. I never looked back. It meant really leaning down, but this realism turned into peace of mind.

Misrepresentation

"The States has the best advertising and marketing system in the world. This is rapidly spilling over into other countries", says Darryl. "It's based on control, mis-representation and non-disclosure. People are told: "It's the LAW" when it's really manipulation to keep you spending and accounting to the government. But most people swallow it and remain silent because they think they're powerless.

"Companies send out their terms and conditions in such fine, pale print, in decorative packets grouped together with a lot of colorful promotional material. When you receive your 'contract' in the mail (if you receive it at all) you glance at it, thinking it is just more promotional junk mail and throw it out.

"Terms and conditions are not clearly marked 'Contract' in large enough print that is easy to read. Because if you read it, you would cancel immediately. Then you receive their shocker of a bill with all the tacked on 'hidden charges' their sales people never told you about".

Who's In Control?

Darryl continues, "People have to stand back and say, 'Who's really in control here?' If you think about it, the telephone company, the gas company, city, state and local governments really control your purse strings. The government tells you, "This is what you need to get wealth. I'll take care of you and make you wealthy. I won't let you fall through the safety net. I *am* your safety net". What they're *really* doing is taking your wealth and draining you. I know, I worked for them".

The 'Cult' Of Government Is To Break Your Sprit

"The government has intruded on our lives so much that we don't have time to do anything but *account* to them. By the time we're finished, we're too exhausted to object. *That's a key part of their plan: to overload and exhaust you and break your spirit.* When you break a person's spirit, you've got them. *This is the cult of government.* But government bodies have no power that we haven't given them. We can get our power back by grouping together and saying 'No'".

A Bank Manager's Integrity

Tom Porter is an account executive for **Western Bank**, a small family owned bank in Minnesota that offers personal service. Tom has a high profile. He's been in banking all of his life and radiates the unmistakable good will of someone who enjoys his job. He's often invited to foreign countries to give talks and advice on modern banking. He also talks to schools, large corporations and other organizations.

Tom Had A Conflict

"I quit working for a huge U.S. bank because I just couldn't live with myself. I watched the bank spend enormous amounts of money marketing their customers to use ATM cards instead of writing checks or cashing them at the bank. They convinced their customers that ATM cards would save them time and money. After heavy marketing, their customers finally 'swallowed the bait' and began using their ATM cards.

"ATM cards didn't benefit the customer at all. I saw customers over spending and getting themselves into financial binds because cards made getting cash too easy. The *real* reason behind the bank's marketing campaign was hugely profitable for the bank. Processing money electronically cut down on time, paperwork and reduced staff.

"But that wasn't enough. Once the bank had convinced their customers to use ATM cards, they started *charging* them for using them to *double their profits*. I couldn't live with this greed-based misrepresentation. I quit".

Penalized For Saving

Tom continues, "People don't consistently save. Most governments don't encourage them to do so. In fact, they penalize them for saving by taxing them on the interest they earn. On one hand, people are taxed for earning, then they're taxed for saving. As a result only 2% of the American population seriously saves.

"To penalize people for trying to become financially stable and secure is in my opinion immoral and an infringement on their civil liberties. This is why 80% of the wealth of this country is now held off shore.

Keep A Tight Reign On Credit Cards

"As a banker I have watched for years how people get themselves into trouble financially. By far the biggest seduction is using credit cards. People go out and buy things on their cards they don't have money for and run up enormous bills which they pay high interest on. I've seen it ruin their happiness and their health. There are many people who *never* use credit cards and do just fine".

You Can Do Fine

Remember, you can take care of yourself. You can save $1,000 very easily, you don't need a large bank to lend it to you, but that's become the way we think. It's marketing. 'If you need money, go to the bank'. In the past if you needed money, you saved it. You can start that good habit again. It will give you renewed self respect and a feeling of control. If you're fed up with 'Big Brother' and 'The System' the following Mental Picturing techniques will help you take back your control and ease them out of your life.

Demolish 'The System'

We all resent rules, regulations and endless red-tape that erode our precious time and hard earned wealth. What's more, we *pay* bureaucrats through our taxes to tell us what to do. It's absurd. Try this: picture a big, imposing building with a plaque named 'The System' on it's door then see a huge bulldozer drive up and clear it all away. Remember you're mentally bulldozing in order to demolish a disempowering concept, you're not hurting anyone physically.

When the bulldozer's done, picture a huge pile of 'Freedom And Wealth' where the building *was*. Next, see people *peacefully* come up and take what they want. There's no pushing, shoving or fighting. There's plenty for everyone. You do the same. Walk up to the 'Freedom And Wealth' pile and help yourself. *Feel* the peaceful atmosphere that prevails once 'The System' is gone. Affirm, "The System no longer runs my life. I'm free".

Send 'Big Brother' Packing

This next technique most people enjoy. Send 'Big Brother' packing. Imagine there's an unfriendly, overbearing bully in your home, ordering you around. He's carrying a briefcase with the words 'Big Brother' written on it. He's telling you all the things you have to account to him for. His list is *endless* and he threatens that if you don't do as he says, you'll be in *deep trouble*.

Tell 'Big Brother', "Thanks but no thanks. I'm on to you and can take care of myself just fine. Now get out! And furthermore, I'm not paying you to tell me what to do anymore".

See 'Big Brother' turn purple with rage as you calmly walk to your front door, open it and show him out. Hear him splutter, "Well, I never! You'll be sorry". Reply, "No I won't. *You're* the one who's going to be sorry. You're *fired*. You're nothing but a pain in the neck and I'm not supporting you anymore. OUT"!

'Big Brother' stomps out of your front door and *disappears. Feel* the pleasure of knowing you *never* have to be bothered by him again. Affirm, 'Big Brother' is gone forever". Feel the pleasure and *freedom* that you're now your own boss and can call your own shots.

You can keep all the balls in the air.

Chapter Seven

Back-Up Your Success

Back-up techniques are your best insurance. When you've finished your Mental Picturing, back-up techniques will put the frosting on the cake. They're like a lock and key. They'll lock the picturing you've done firmly into your subconscious mind.

One Important Thing

There's one thing that *will* slow your Mental Picturing down. That's when you want something, you picture it and then immediately decide 'how' you're going to get it, or *how* it has to happen.

This book *is* about using your mind to take the steps that lead to success. But the *secret* is to *let your subconscious mind do the talking* through inspiring ideas and keep your *conscious* mind *quiet*.

A Great Work Horse

Your conscious, every day mind is a great work horse. It handles your daily activities, keeps your books straight, arrives at your appointments on time, or *early, (if you aren't early for an appointment, you're late)* and makes great practical decisions. Your conscious mind prioritizes your actions and makes the best use of your time and energy. But it will *never* inspire you. Your subconscious does this.

Your subconscious mind is your 'magic carpet' that flies you to your next perfect step. You have to listen to your subconscious very carefully. Listen, get your inspiration and then act. Fast!

Become Quiet

There are so many creative short cuts to help you achieve your goals. Just because you decide on a goal and picture it, don't go wildly out and try to force it to happen. Haven't you tried to force something to happen, or make someone do something for you and it just doesn't work? Then suddenly the very thing you want, happens in a totally different way?

Keep An Open Mind

For your mental picturing to work, you have to be open-minded and receptive to inspiration. This doesn't mean you won't work like blazes once the inspiration hits you. But, you have to do your picturing and then let the inspiration come to you *naturally*. This can happen very quickly, *(and you'll know when it's a right idea)*; but also, it could take weeks or a month to trigger the idea that's your next perfect step. Be patient.

So Many Ways

There're so many ways life can bring good luck to you. We never know except in hindsight how things will work out. That's one of the most enjoyable parts of Mental Picturing. Good luck can come from a chance meeting or someone we depend on. But if we decide, "this is *how,* and this is *who* is going to deliver for me", we slow ourselves down. Crack the nut of 'How' and see how quickly the opportunities present themselves.

Crack A New Nut

This Mental Picturing technique is so simple you'll depend on it for *any* situation. It will *quiet* your conscious mind so you can hear the inspiration of your subconscious. You're going to crack a new nut of 'How'. Then the short cuts you want will start rolling in. This is how it goes: once you've finished Mental Picturing for something you want, close your eyes and picture a nut with the word 'How' written on it and then crack it. Crack the nut of 'How' for each goal you've pictured. For example, if you want a new home, picture living in it, then crack the nut of 'How'. Or, perhaps you want to clear your debts, see your bank balance in credit, then crack the nut of 'How', and so on. You'll never regret using this back-up technique. I think it's one of the most important one's you can do.

Why Go For It When 'It' Can Come To You?

You may be surprised at how ingenious some of the ideas your subconscious gives you are. You can also be surprised that when you've been picturing for something and crack the nut of 'How' what you want *comes to you*, instead of you having to chase after *it*.

The telephone may ring and someone you've wanted to help you will just 'be there' when you never thought this could happen. Use this technique often and it will produce results that make creating wealth much easier.

Watch Inspiring Videos

I can't stress how careful you have to be about *not* filling your mind with doom and gloom. The information you put in your mind is like the food you eat. It will make you strong or weak.

Stop reading horror stories in the newspapers, be very selective about what you watch on television and the 'thrillers' you read. You just cannot afford to use your mental energy to absorb violence or hard luck stories. Once a negative impression is taken in by your mind it will come out somewhere in your life.

Feed Yourself With Inspiration

My clients watch inspiring videos when they need a break. I do too. These are the ones we seem to like best.

Working Girl is a favorite, because 'Tess', the heroine is very bright, but she couldn't get ahead in the stock market because she didn't have the background or formal education to be taken seriously.

Yet the people Tess worked for *always* took her seriously. She was ambitious and followed the market carefully and came up with a lot of 'bright ideas'. Her bosses knew she was bright, but instead of giving her credit or a chance to get ahead, they stole her ideas and made money off them for themselves.

A Leap Of Faith

Finally, Tess found out she was being used and took a

leap of faith. She ran a cliff-hanging risk to take one of her own ideas back and capitalize on it. She won. Not only did she land the deal of the century, but a great job and partner to boot.

Another popular video is **Forrest Gump**. Some laugh at Forrest Gump because they think he's a moron. But Forrest Gump was dumb like a fox. He had something you and I could use, a complete openness to new ideas and the ability to adapt to any situation and cooperate.

Forrest was completely free from ego. His ability to see the best in people and *not judge negatively* always paid off. He was honest, always kept his word, was always protected from the worst and received many honors. He also made pots of money and generously shared his wealth. You and I can learn from Forrest.

Babe is another. An inspiring story of a traditional 'belt and braces' English farmer who takes a leap of faith on a pig he won at a rural fair. The farmer soon recognizes that this is no ordinary pig, but one with *extraordinary* talents.

'Pig' who was at first earmarked as the main course for the farmer's Christmas dinner turned out to be an ace sheep-herding-pig. On an irrational 'whim' this traditional farmer trained 'Pig' and entered him in the sheep dog trials. Everyone thought the farmer had lost his marbles but 'Pig' *won*. One can't help but be touched by this courageous, outrageous movie.

White Fang is another favorite. It's about two fellows who strike it rich in the Gold Rush Days in the Klondike in Alaska. They don't just strike it rich, they strike it *seriously* rich. The two work hard to adjust to one another and become working companions. It was hard work, but it paid off. They became close friends.

The Lion King is a movie everyone, adults and children love. It has to be one of the most inspiring stories ever about growing into maturity, taking responsibility and having courage. It's also visually beautiful and full of inspiring music. So when you need a boost these are some videos that could help.

Music Calms The Soul

Hard rock can hype you up, but beautiful music will help you calm down. Sound is very important to your state of mind. Have you ever noticed how you feel when the air hammers are out, tearing up the road in front of your house? If you're working hard it can make you want to tear your hair out.

You need music that will help you concentrate on your goals. Listening to lovely music playing in the background while you work or drive to an appointment will do you a lot of good.

Scientific tests have proven that plants grow faster and stronger when gentle music is played in the lab. On the other hand, when they're exposed to harsh music or sounds they get stunted and wilt. The same goes for you. Think about it.

Keep All The Balls In The Air

Becoming a 'Juggler' is a Mental Picturing technique that will help you keep all the balls in the air and not get stressed-out. When you're going for success, you're going to be multi-tasking until you are blue in the face. You're doing everything yourself until you can afford to have people help you. You just have to do it. But there's a bonus. *The more you do for yourself the freer you are.*

Is there anything worse than teaming up with a partner who lets you down? The time, energy and money you waste in disappointment and freeing yourself from the relationship can take a heavy toll on you — not just emotionally but on your check book. There's a bonus in doing it all yourself. You'll learn the hands-on skills of running your business, so if others let you down, so what? You can do it yourself. This is freedom. It's also power. Try this next technique:

Become A Juggler

Relax, close your eyes and imagine you're a juggler. The kind you see at fun fairs. You're juggling several balls in the air and you're doing this *effortlessly*. *Feel* the pleasure of keeping all the balls in the air with a smile on your face.

In the next chapter you are going to learn the secrets of Wealthy People. You will probably be able to add to this list with secrets of your own. Decide now to become wealthy and never look back.

Shop around before you buy.

Chapter Eight

Wealthy People's Secrets

All the wealthy, healthy, successful, happy people I've interviewed for this book consider the following points essential to success. Some points are self-evident while others, like saving wisely, pushing your vision, learning how to avoid buying mistakes and the strength of the family we'll explore in more detail. First, the secrets.

Secrets

1. Make your money by *inspiration*, not by the sweat of your brow. It will still be *plenty of work,* but when you're fired with enthusiasm, it's more fun.

2. Take total responsibility for your financial situation and start cleaning it up immediately.

3. Decide to be *wealthy*, not just rich. This means appreciating, enjoying and taking care of what you have, no matter how modest. If you want to upgrade it, do this through Mental Picturing first, and you'll attract new opportunities to become wealthy.

4. Stop 'selling' your customers and start *inspiring* them. If you inspire people, they'll buy. You do this by working at something you enjoy and believe in.

5. Set clear goals and go for your 'This is it'! If you don't know what you want, make a list of everything you *don't* want, and work up from there.

6. Create multiple strings of income, so if one source goes flat for a while, you still have money coming in from others. Remember Vidal Sasoon who created a line a products that 'paid him to sleep'?

7. Take plenty of professional advice. It will save you money and sleepless nights. Source consumer organizations and groups of people who are on your wave length, will support you and *group* with them.

8. Keep your books straight and up to date.

9. Pay your bills on time, and if possible *pay them early*. The quicker you pay the more relaxed you'll feel and you'll build good-will and good credit.

10. Create products or services that improve the quality of life for others and make *them* wealthy too.

11. Stay in good physical health. Your earning capacity is dependent on your energy. If you're teetering on burn out, lighten-up and give yourself a break. Relaxing and getting your mind off business will make the solutions you seek obvious.

12. Develop inter-dependent, not dependent, working relationships. That way, if someone you're working with lets you down, you can still get the job done yourself, it may just take a little longer.

13. Extricate yourself from 'The System' and 'Big Brother' in every possible way. Cut out products and services that trap you like direct debit, call waiting, high car and mortgage payments. Cut up your credit cards if necessary. You won't miss them.

14. Simplify your life and working methods by putting things away where they belong, *right away*. You'll save 50% more time that you now spend looking for things. You may be in such a rush to succeed that you don't have time to put things away.

15. When you start a project, don't stop until you've finished it. Then go on to the next. Completing a project will give you self-respect, balance, and confidence about your 'next step'.

16. Start saving money, early and consistently. Try to take 10% of what you earn and put it away.

17. Get an E-Mail address, it will save you time, energy and money. It's also a lot of fun.

18. Never pay an unfair bill. Settle what you feel is fair and do it quickly.

19. Make purchases based on the benefits they will give you, not what they cost. You may be able to buy a pair of shoes for $20, but if the $80 pair makes you look like a million, they're an *investment*.

20. Value your family, they're your best supporters. Whenever possible, involve them in your business.

21. Never forget, *the more you do for yourself the freer you are*. You don't have to put up with, or *pay for* other people's incompetence. No one cares more about getting the job done right than you do.

22. Say "Thank You" and *do* "Thank You" by sharing your knowledge and supporting others who are trying to make a positive contribution. The more you share the more you get.

23. Give yourself *permission* to be wealthy! Obnoxious people have fortunes. Do they deserve it? Don't hold back on allowing yourself money until you deserve it. Decide to have it now whether you deserve it or not. It's a choice.

23. Be compassionate with yourself. If a personal hardship lands you in debt over your head, consider asking your creditors to settle for a portion of it. They will receive tax relief on your bad debt, and you can roll up your sleeves and start afresh without breaking your own spirit.

Save Wisely, Early And Consistently

Tom Porter of Western Bank said the best advice he could give people who want to become financially free are two things: "save money early, consistently and if you don't have it, don't spend it.

"The best way to save" says Tom, "is to open up a savings account in a bank that is *very inconvenient* to get to. That way you aren't tempted to go and take money out. It's just too much trouble. Arrange to have the money you save taken *directly* out of your paycheck and deposited into your savings account. Then live on what's left. Even if the tax-man stings you for saving, my advice is to save anyway and start early when you're 20 or 21. If you do this, you can retire much earlier".

If You Don't Have It, Don't Spend It

"My wife and I made a decision from day one that if we wanted to buy something, for example a new television, we only bought it if we had the money for it. We didn't use our credit cards. We cut back on other things until we got the money together. When we had enough, we went out and bought the television and really enjoyed it knowing we owned it free and clear".

Don't Pay For Using ATM Cards

Tom continues, "ATM machines abound these days and are charging increasing fees just to use them to get cash. Our bank has a policy to never charge our customers for using ATM cards. Even if you have to drive to the bank your card is drawn on, do so. You shouldn't have to pay a fee and you'll feel better and more in control for not allowing yourself to be 'stung'".

Get Behind And 'Push'

The more you do for yourself the freer and wealthier you will be. Also, the more you do for yourself the more others will support you.

Crispin Tweddell, the Chairman of **Piper Trust**, is a brilliant entrepreneur. He runs a highly respected private U.K. company that invests in other people's projects. Crispin said, "Whenever we receive a business plan from a company that says, "If we had the money we would do this", we throw it straight in the trash.

"On the other hand when we receive a business plan from a small company that is doing it anyway, that's one we'll support. Whether we enter their picture or not, they're going to grow their vision. With our support they could be more successful, improve the quality of people's lives and help both our company's prosper. Those are people we support".

Crispin continued, "Look at it this way, if your car breaks down and you stand in the road and say, "If I had a tow truck, I would move my car. Well, if you don't have one, you get behind and push. When you do, someone usually comes along and helps. It's the companies who are pushing that interest us".

Avoid Buying Mistakes

Is there anything worse than impulse buying (especially on credit), only to take your purchase home and realize it's not right, or that you don't really like it after all? Now you're going to learn a secret that will give you tremendous pleasure in your purchases and help you avoid buying mistakes. It goes without saying that by now, you will have become a 'Mental Picturer'. This skill will pay off in *every* area of your life.

Shop Around

When you want to buy something shop *thoroughly* but don't buy. Shop *everywhere*. Look at *everything*, <u>comb</u> the stores, but don't buy. Do a good shopping then go home, drop the whole idea and go about your normal routine. Nine times out of ten you'll get a vivid picture in your mind about what to buy, then you can go and buy it with confidence.

This is how all my clients 'shop'. I do too. For example, the other day there were several things I *thought* I needed for my office and home. I combed the stores, looked at things, talked with people but didn't buy. Then I went home and dropped the whole idea of buying and fixed supper. I just forgot about 'buying'.

When I was washing the dishes, a very clear picture came into my mind of a green second-hand vase I'd found in a thrift shop. The next day I went and bought it, and it turned out to be just the ticket for a plant I wanted to pot for my office. It has added a lot of beauty to my office and cost me exactly $2.

Try shopping like this and you'll be amazed at how it works. You won't waste money on extras you don't need right now or end up feeling guilty about making buying mistakes *when every penny counts*.

Frequent Thrift Shops

People often feel only the poor buy at thrift shops. Forget it. Smart people buy at thrift shops. If you know what you're looking for and can spot a good bargain you can beautifully furnish your home, office and even find nice clothes at thrift shops for very little. This doesn't mean you have to buy *everything* there, but don't sell thrift shops or auction rooms short.

The objects you buy at thrift shops were donated by people who care about sharing. Some people couldn't care less. They just throw their useless (even expensive) things away, whereas donated items are given by people who care. Think about it.

Make Purchases Based On Their Real Value

Sometimes you'll need to buy expensive new items

because they're an investment. We often buy things because they're cheap. Other times, we buy expensive things that we think make us feel or look rich. When buying anything analyze, "What is this going to *do* for me? How can it *support* me in achieving my goals? You may need to spend some serious money on a few good clothes. If your clothes are 'down at the heel' you're not going to make a very good impression.

'All business is show business' is a well known saying. You may need to improve your show. This doesn't mean you have to go crazy and buy a lot of expensive clothes, but a good looking jacket, suit or a new pair of shoes could make a big difference in the impression you make. People notice missing buttons, soiled ties, unpolished, worn out shoes and things like that. The reverse is also true. Even if your clothes are old, if they are clean and tidy and your shoes are polished, you will make a good impression.

The Strength Of The Family

Value your family. Darryl McKinnon says, "Becoming financially free is not a matter of doing what's hard or doing what's easy. It's a matter of doing what's right. When you do what's right you go to sleep with a clear conscience.

"Our forefathers had the answer. Our country worked then because the *family* was in control, and the community worked together. If someone's barn burned down, everyone pulled together and rebuilt it. They did it out of generosity and genuine caring. They took responsibility not just for themselves but for their community. We've lost our self-sufficiency because we have lost our sense of community and devotion to our family. We should be grouping together the way our forefathers did.

"There is a community of honest people out there. We just have to find each other and group together. Doing this is worth *everything*. We each have our own unique talents which we can share and support each other with. That's community. It's also 'family'".

The real Treasure Island is in your mind.

Chapter Nine

Treasure Island

The following is a *Journey In Imagination*. I put one in all of my books. It is an *imaginary* journey and is a *far-fetched* use of your imagination. It should be used *as a tool* to trigger ideas in your own mind about how you can achieve a ready supply of money *through your own efforts* without hocking yourself to the hilt.

For example, remember how I described 'Winning The Lottery' on page 67 and how your odds of winning are less than being struck by lightning? Well this is the same. But just like the lottery, by Mentally Picturing this 'far-fetched' imaginary 'Journey' you'll wake up your mind to creative things you can do that will lead you to financial freedom. First, I'll describe it so you can get a feeling for it. Then on page 135 you'll 'Take A Journey' to experience it deeply. Here goes:

Standing In The Sunset

You're standing on the beach in the sunset, gazing at an island close to shore. The island you're looking at is your own *private* island. No one can see it or get there but you, so don't worry about robbers and thieves coming in and robbing you blind. It's your island. Only *you* can see it or get there. It's called Treasure Island.

You stand on the shore, gazing at your island and breathing in the smell of the sea. A soft breeze blows and you can hear the sound of seagulls circling overhead. Right now, you need some money, so you're going to hop in your motor boat, visit your island and collect some.

Your boat is tied to a pier that you *also* own. It is neat, new and fast and has a motor so you don't have to struggle with rowing. You leap in, switch on the motor and your boat takes off.

Easily and quickly you steer your boat to your private island, pull up to the shore, tie your boat to a little pier and get out and stroll over your island just for the pleasure of it. It's *beautiful.*

It's like a paradise. Full of swaying palms and money trees. The sand is soft and damp under your feet, and scattered with sparkling diamonds, precious gems and gold that you can scoop up. Does this sound impossible? Read on.

Your Imagination Does It All

We all need to *permanently* establish financial freedom for ourselves and those we love in order to feel *peace of mind*. This 'Journey' will help you do this by firing-up your imagination to see how to achieve this. It will do more by helping you *experience* your *real* goals and your *real* priorities, not those that 'society' says you need to 'fit in'. You need to find your *own* quality of life that brings you fulfillment and a sense of 'This is it'! For each of us it's different.

You Can Become Free

Sometimes we feel we just can't win. Don't believe it. In your imagination you can. History is full of stories of people who were 'written-off' as failures. Henry Ford and his 'horseless carriage' was one of them. Henry's strong desire and belief in what he was doing not only enabled him to 'make it' but enriched the quality of all our lives through his motorcars.

This 'Journey' to Treasure Island will help you discover your 'This is it'! so you can enrich yourself and others through work that inspires you. *Remember, the real 'Treasure Island' is in your mind.* There is *nothing* your mind cannot do, no 'miracle' it cannot pull off when you practice Mental Picturing. It will always give you new-found self-confidence, pride and put you firmly in the driver's seat if you give it a good chance.

Your future is *not* predetermined. Nor, is there a heavy hand of fate holding you back to a hard, joyless life. You can create financial freedom and escape the grip of fate through the world of your imagination. Through Mental Picturing you can create a financial future that conforms to your dreams instead of your fears.

All the good things you have in your life right now started with a desire, a wish or a dream. Then your imagination got fired-up and made it a reality. Now you're going to use your imagination to fulfill your desire for financial freedom and begin to live the life you wish for, not the one you worry you might have to settle for. Remember, this is *your* 'Journey' and it's *your* financial future. Go for your Treasure Island.

I'm now going to describe a scene to you which is imaginary. It's a relaxed, vivid and beautiful scene that you'll follow in your imagination. It's like taking a trip, but instead of travelling in an airplane or a car you will travel in your imagination. *The words and images are often repeated to produce an emotional response in you.* So don't think too hard or try to figure things out. Just relax and experience the feelings, pictures, sounds, colors and scents as much as possible These gentle experiences will act as signposts to your subconscious mind and show you how to achieve the financial freedom you want.

Read through your 'Journey' slowly. It's a meditation. If you wish, you can make an audio tape of this Journey using your own voice for your own use. If you picture scenes that are different from those I'm describing, that's *fine*. Let your imagination take you where it wants. It has things to show you and help you to understand.

In order to deeply relax, draw your curtains, sit down, put your feet up and switch off your phone. If you can stay awake while you're lying down, feel free to stretch out. If you don't have time to do this, don't worry. You'll get plenty of benefit from listening to Treasure Island while washing the dishes, getting ready for work, cleaning your car or dropping off to sleep. If you wake up in the middle of the night, read through your 'Journey' or listen to it on tape. You may be surprised how quickly you fall back to sleep. You may even have vivid, informative dreams.

Relax And 'Journey'

Now, take a couple of deep breaths and allow yourself to begin to relax and let go. It's a *wonderful* feeling to relax. Allow the relaxation to begin moving through your body. Let it move into your feet, relaxing them completely, then into your ankles and calves and next your knees and thighs. Feel the relaxation moving into your pelvic area, your abdominal region and then gently filling your chest, arms and back.

Let the feeling of relaxation completely overtake you now as it moves up into your neck, your head, relaxing your forehead, cheeks, jaw, the muscles around your mouth and your eyelids. Feel your whole body begin to let go and relax with a sense of stillness and peace.

On this 'Journey' to Treasure Island you'll experience the freedom of being financially free, *forever.* You're going to travel into a future where you'll experience the quality of life you've always wanted. A quality of life that brings you happiness and pride. Remember, this is your 'Journey', it's your Treasure Island and it's *your* future. You're free to experience it any way you want.

Take another couple of deep breaths and imagine how it would feel to *own* your own private island of money which no one can see or get to but you. Your swift boat takes you to your island, you pull up to the shore and get out. The sand on your island isn't sand, it's *gold dust*. The sea shells and rocks sprinkled on the sand are made of precious gems, diamonds, rubies, emeralds, sapphires. pearls and pure gold. The trees sway in the breeze. They're *money trees.*

The smell of the sea and sound of the surf are deeply relaxing. Dramatic rocks and boulders make your island beautiful. You look closely at these enormous rocks and see they're layered, like the dessert 'mille feuilles'. The layers are made of gold, silver and crisp, new bank notes that *easily* break off in huge chunks.

You wander around your island, just for the fun of it, admiring it's wealth and beauty *knowing* that it's *yours.* You pick up some of the precious gems that sprinkle the beach and examine them. They're beautiful.

Now, walk over to one of the huge rocks and break off several chunks of money. The wonderful part is that you don't have to take it all, in fact you *couldn't* there's so much. The light-weight carry-all you've brought with you opens easily and you fill it to the brim. Once your carry-all is full, you take another stroll over your beautiful island for the pleasure of it and know it's yours. Your Treasure Island. Your carry-all full, now you get back in your boat and make your way back to the mainland. As you travel you look over your shoulder at your Treasure Island which is beautifully silhouetted in a radiant sky. This is your own private island. Remember no one can see it, steal from it or visit it but you. Upon arriving at the mainland, you tie up your boat and then go buy whatever you want. *Feel* the gratitude of knowing you have an *endless supply of money*.

Journey Regularly

By taking this journey on a regular basis to Treasure Island, you'll begin to experience a new feeling of hope, determination and control in your life and see how you can achieve the goals you most desire.

Back-up your 'Journey' with affirmations like the ones described in the next chapter. For example: affirm: "I have my own *private* Treasure Island that no one can touch or approach but me", or "I have an endless supply of money that nothing can *ever* take from me".

Financial freedom is possible. Others have achieved it,

why not you? Everything good that you have right now started with a dream and a desire to have more out of life. Then you made it a reality. You can make financial freedom happen the same way. Remember, you can come back to your Treasure Island as often as you want, any time you want and take this 'Journey' to re-commit to the financial freedom you desire.

Now, you'll return to the place where you started your journey, remembering everything you experienced. Soon you'll find yourself back in the place where you started your journey, fully alert and able to clearly remember all the details.

This imaginary journey is your key to contacting your subconscious mind and to creating wealth for yourself. It will help you to write down the high points you experienced in your 'Journey' in a special book, so you can picture these regularly. By taking this journey every day for a week, then 2-3 times in the second week and once a week thereafter, you'll become focused and strong in your resolve. Remember, feel free to record this 'Journey' using your own voice for your own use for a deeper experience. If you wish, you can order a pre-recorded version from Touchstone Publications.

Give yourself permission to be financially free.

Chapter Ten

Brainwash Yourself

This book is to show you how to create a great life for yourself, not 'just a living'. Positive affirmations will support you in doing this. *They are the way you tell yourself the truth in advance.*

You're learning Mental Picturing to change your mindset so you will think *well* of yourself and feel you can have a better life and become *wealthy*. Affirmations are things you say or think about yourself, life or other people. When they're positive, they will back-up the new life you're picturing for yourself and those you love. When they're negative, they do just the opposite.

Whatever you do, stop telling yourself, "That's too good for me" or, "I'll never make it" or "I'm not one of the lucky ones", because you'll *un-do* your Mental Picturing. *Affirmations become self-fulfilling prophesies.*

Why The Downers?

The reason we put ourselves down is because we think if we don't expect much from life, we won't be disappointed when we don't get it. Life can be full of success. Yes, it will have it's disappointments. All I can say is that Mental Picturing will up-grade your outlook on life *and* your bank account. Following-up Mental Picturing with positive affirmations is an extra-help.

Self-Talk

An affirmation is not a question, it's a *statement*. "I'll never make it" is a negative affirmation. "I'm making it" is a positive affirmation.

Believe The Best

You always believe something. Why not believe the best? You believe you can or cannot have things. You believe you can or cannot do things If you believe you can't, your subconscious will help you. If you believe you can, it will help you here. Your wealth and happiness depend on believing the *best*. The way you seal-in the good effects of your Mental Picturing is through positive affirmations.

Say your affirmations silently or out loud so often that you start to *believe* them. Don't expect to believe them overnight, that's expecting too much. One vitamin pill won't give you energy when you've been exhausted for months. Neither will one affirmation. You need to say them regularly to believe them.

Sometimes it helps to affirm your problems as if they were in the past. For example: "I used to be irresponsible but now I'm focused", or "I used to be untidy, but now I'm neat as a pin". Both you, and your subconscious can accept these realistic, hopeful statements.

What if you feel like a complete crumb of the earth and can't find anything positive about yourself? Think. There must be *something* you're good at? Maybe you're a great cook, an excellent driver or gardener. The more you acknowledge your good points, no matter how insignificant, the more you'll find about yourself to admire. For example, maybe you're a loving father or mother. If you affirm these positive points about yourself, gradually you'll start to think, "Well, maybe I'm not so bad after all". *When you acknowledge your good points, you're on your way home.*

The rest of this chapter sets out a combination of affirmations. Mix and match them in any way you enjoy, and make many more of your own. You can write your affirmations in a special book, say them silently or out loud, or record them on tape using your own voice. Say or listen to your affirmations anytime, anywhere: while driving, getting ready for work or dropping off to sleep.

Brainwashing yourself with positive affirmations is one of the kindest things you can do for yourself. Good luck!

Independence

The more I do for myself, the freer I am.

'Big Brother' and 'The System' are gone from my life.

I can take care of myself just fine.

I'm my own boss and call my own shots.

The 'Rug Puller' is gone from my life forever.

Inspiration

My mind is open and clear to inspiring ideas.

My mind is like a magic carpet that flies me to success.

Money flows to me as easily as fresh air.

I'm standing on a pot of gold at the end of a rainbow.

I own an orchard of money trees and 'rake it in'.

Success

Life goes to the courageous.

Being successful is a 'full time job'. So is being poor.

Life is *not* a win-loss roller coaster, it's a winning circle.

I've stopped seeking, and now choose to find success.

Mouth watering windfalls come my way.

Money

Money is a gift which I use wisely and productively.

I never spend more than I can comfortably earn.

I have endless opportunities to become wealthy.

Money is as plentiful as air.

I never have to worry about money again.

Values

Saying 'Thank You' empowers me and touches others.

I earn the wealth I long for, and have stopped waiting for anyone else to give it to me.

I _____value peace of mind and quality of life.

I _____ value people who inspire others.

I _____ wish to become the best that I can be.

I buy things for their *value*, not because of their price.

Goals

Yes I, _____ want this.

No, this is not that important. I don't need it.

I follow up on my no-doubt-about-it goals.

My priorities are straight. I've found my 'This is it'!

I up-grade my quality of life every day.

Wealth

I own my own home free and clear in a fine neighborhood with friendly neighbors.

Being wealthy is a peaceful state of mind. Money is just money.

Even if I'm short of money, I can *always* be wealthy.

I _____can be wealthy and still be a good person.

Being wealthy is a full time job, but it's an inspiring one.

I make my money by INSPIRATION, not by the sweat of my brow.

Resources

Contacting Julia Hastings

Julia is always happy to hear from you. If you would like to share your success story, thoughts or questions about Mental Picturing she would be happy to write you. For prompt mail order of books, tapes, information about one-to-one coaching and seminars, write to Julia at:

Touchstone Publications
www.You-Have-What-It-Takes.com, or E-Mail:
Julia @ You-Have-What-It-Takes.com

Recommended Reading

You may like to read other books that relate to wealth, happiness and financial freedom. These are some we have found very helpful:

Life Is Tremendous, by Charlie 'Tremendous' Jones, available from **Life Management Services,** 206 West Allen Street, Mechanicsburg, PA 17055, USA., Tel: 1-800-233-2665, Fax: 1-717-766-6565. *Deeply inspiring.*

Living The Simple Life, by Elaine St. James, available through **Hyperion** books, New York, USA. *Wonderful.*

The Power Of Positive Thinking, by Dr. Norman Vincent Peale, available through, **Fawcett Crest**, New York, USA. A classic book on positive thinking.

Money Troubles: Legal Strategies To Cope With Your Debts, available through **Nolo Press**, USA., l997, Tel: 800-992 6656. Excellent, comprehensive information.

Mortgage Free, *Radical Strategies For Home Ownership*, Rob Roy, Chelsea Green Publishing Company, White River Junction Vermont, USA, 1998, 800-639-4099, www.chelseagreen.com. *You can own your home.*

The Better Business Bureau has offices all over the USA.

The Citizens Advice Bureau's Money Advice Trust and **National Debtline Service** in the U.K. offers excellent and comprehensive advice on every money problem.

People Mentioned In This Book

If you wish to contact any of the people mentioned in this book their addresses are:

Tom Porter, **Western Bank,** P. O. Box 6469, St. Paul, Mn., 55164, USA, E-Mail: edie@usinternet.com

Darryl McKinnon, **Metropolitan Publishing**, P.O. Box, 582762, Mpls. Mn., USA, 55458-2752, E-mail: metrobooks@aol.com

Michael Wolff, **Ki Net Business Information**, Dower House, Lethen, Nairn IV12 5PR, Scotland UK, Tel/Fax: (44) 1667 452123, E-mail: mwolff@ki-net.co.uk, Web Site: http://www.ki-net.co.uk

Crispin Tweddell, Chairman, **Piper Trust**, Eardley House, 182 - 184 Campden Hill Road, London W8 7AS, Tel: (44) 171 727 3866, Fax: (44) 171 727 8969, E-mail: crispin@pipertrust.co.uk

Coaching In Mental Picturing

If you are interested in one-to-one coaching in Mental Picturing with Julia Hastings, this coaching is geared at high-achievers. It's also for those who are ready to make the leap into a fuller career or more committed personal lifestyle.

Mental Picturing Is An Old Sport

Mental picturing first became known when the East German and Russian athletes used it to excel in the Olympics. Golfer's, footballer's and skier's are known mental picturers'. This technique is now being used in sports, business, health care and education. The use of mental picturing to accelerate the attainment of goals is unparalleled.

You Are Always Picturing

"How often do you say "I knew it"! when something turns out the way you thought it would? Without realizing it, you are rehearsing an event *before* it happens. This is mental picturing".

You Can Have What You Want © Julia Hastings

The problem is, we often picture events we worry might happen instead of using our imagination to focus on events we want to have happen. Mental picturing will teach you how to do this. It will give you the tools to achieve a seamless transition to peak performance. If one-to-one coaching is of interest to you, contact Julia through **www.You-Have-What-It-Takes.com.** You can download preliminary information, then E-Mail Julia if you think it's for you.

Other Books And Tapes By Julia Hastings

Julia Hastings specializes in teaching mental picturing. Her books and tapes have been translated into seven foreign languages. Books do not repeat her tapes, but work hand-in-hand as powerful tools for change.

Book - You Can Have What You Want, beautifully designed with 10 full paged cartoons shows you how to succeed in relationships, money and health. "You don't have to settle for second best, you can have what you want". This book will show you how. $12.95

Tape - Your New Self Image co-ordinates with **You Can Have What You Want.** Your self-image is what you think you are. It's also what you feel others think about you. Side 1 explains mental picturing. On side 2 you'll take a relaxing *Journey In Imagination* and change your self-image for the new one you want. 55 min. $12.95

Book - You're Great!, *Three Steps To Self-Confidence* Self confidence comes from one thing: doing your 'This is it!' the activity that will bring you deep happiness. Beautifully designed with many full paged cartoons and a chapter on self-confidence and sex appeal, this book will give you unshakable self-confidence that no one can take away. $12.95

Tape - The Butterfly of Happiness co-ordinates with **You're Great!** Happiness is like a butterfly. If you chase after it, it will always be just beyond your grasp. If you become quiet and still, it will fly down and alight on you. Side 1 shows how happiness is doing what you love. If you're not sure what you want, side two's *Journey In Imagination* will help you find out. 55 min. $12.95

Book - The Day Dream Diet, *The Inner Game Of Dieting* is a truly inspiring book. Rejuvenate, shape-up and create the future you want through mental picturing. This book will help you succeed on any diet of your choice, and get the upper hand on eating disorders. It's 'Silver Bullets' diet and beauty secrets work like *magic*. You'll recognize the 'The Fat Monster' and get him out of your life *forever*. $15.95

Tape - Creating Your Own Future double audio tapes co-ordinates with **The Day Dream Diet**. We often feel our future is predetermined or that a heavy hand of fate is holding us back. Don't believe it! Side 1 & 2 discuss the 3 steps to creating your own future. Side 3 & 4 take you on a relaxing *Journey In Imagination* where you'll choose the future you want. Because many use *'The Journey'* for sleep or to manage stress, it has been recorded on both sides to save re-winding. 115 min. $l9.99.

Book - How We Did It, *Ordinary People Who Have Done Extraordinary Things Through Mental Picturing* is filled with inspiring, real success stories of people who have done the impossible through Mental Picturing. They've landed jobs, met their mates, made millions and moved to the top even when they were 'written off'. Beautifully designed with over 25 illustrations, this is an inspiring book. $12.95

Tape - Self-Confidence, Self-Esteem & Self-Worth, *You Need Them All!* This single cassette is one of Julia's most popular and coordinates with **How We Did It**. It is also an excellent third tape to go with **You're Great!** You're often told, "Be more self-confident! Have more self-esteem"! But what makes these up? In a group workshop Julia discusses the components of self-confidence and tells an inspiring story of healing. 60 min., $12.95

Special offers on book and tape sets are listed on our Web Site **www.You-Have-What-It-Takes.com**

You can achieve financial freedom.